GLOBALVIEWPOINTS

Suicide

Other Books of Related Interest:

Current Controversies Series

The Elderly

Global Viewpoints Series

Death and Dying

Introducing Issues with Opposing Viewpoints Series

The Death Penalty

Opposing Viewpoints Series

Extremism

GLOBALVIEWPOINTS

Suicide

Margaret Haerens, Book Editor

GREENHAVEN PRESS
A part of Gale, Cengage Learning

GALE
CENGAGE Learning

Detroit • New York • San Francisco • New Haven, Conn • Waterville, Maine • London

Elizabeth Des Chenes, *Managing Editor*

© 2012 Greenhaven Press, a part of Gale, Cengage Learning

Gale and Greenhaven Press are registered trademarks used herein under license.

For more information, contact:
Greenhaven Press
27500 Drake Rd.
Farmington Hills, MI 48331-3535
Or you can visit our Internet site at gale.cengage.com

For product information and technology assistance, contact us at

Gale Customer Support, 1-800-877-4253
For permission to use material from this text or product, submit all requests online at www.cengage.com/permissions

Further permissions questions can be emailed to permissionrequest@cengage.com

Articles in Greenhaven Press anthologies are often edited for length to meet page requirements. In addition, original titles of these works are changed to clearly present the main thesis and to explicitly indicate the author's opinion. Every effort is made to ensure that Greenhaven Press accurately reflects the original intent of the authors. Every effort has been made to trace the owners of copyrighted material.

Cover image © Michael Jenner/Documentary/Corbis.

LIBRARY OF CONGRESS CATALOGING-IN-PUBLICATION DATA

Suicide / Margaret Haerens, book editor.
    p. cm. -- (Global viewpoints)
Summary: "Suicide: Global Suicide Trends; Policies to Address Suicide; Political, Social, and Economic Factors Contributing to Suicide; Suicide As an Act of Terrorism"-- Provided by publisher.
    Includes bibliographical references and index.
    ISBN 978-0-7377-5664-7 (hardback) -- ISBN 978-0-7377-5665-4 (paperback)
    1. Suicide. 2. Suicide--Prevention. 3. Suicide bombings. 4. Terrorism. I. Haerens, Margaret.
    HV6545.S8184 2011
    362.28--dc22
                                                2011015528

Printed in the United States of America
2 3 4 5 6   16 15 14 13 12

Contents

Chapter 1: Global Suicide Trends

Chapter 2: Policies to Address Suicide

Chapter 3: Political, Social, and Economic Factors Contributing to Suicide

Chapter 4: Suicide as an Act of Terrorism

Foreword

"The problems of all of humanity can
only be solved by all of humanity."
—Swiss author Friedrich Dürrenmatt

Global interdependence has become an undeniable reality. Mass media and technology have increased worldwide access to information and created a society of global citizens. Understanding and navigating this global community is a challenge, requiring a high degree of information literacy and a new level of learning sophistication.

Building on the success of its flagship series, Opposing Viewpoints, Greenhaven Press has created the Global Viewpoints series to examine a broad range of current, often controversial topics of worldwide importance from a variety of international perspectives. Providing students and other readers with the information they need to explore global connections and think critically about worldwide implications, each Global Viewpoints volume offers a panoramic view of a topic of widespread significance.

Drugs, famine, immigration—a broad, international treatment is essential to do justice to social, environmental, health, and political issues such as these. Junior high, high school, and early college students, as well as general readers, can all use Global Viewpoints anthologies to discern the complexities relating to each issue. Readers will be able to examine unique national perspectives while, at the same time, appreciating the interconnectedness that global priorities bring to all nations and cultures.

Material in each volume is selected from a diverse range of sources, including journals, magazines, newspapers, nonfiction books, speeches, government documents, pamphlets, organization newsletters, and position papers. Global Viewpoints is truly global, with material drawn primarily from international sources available in English and secondarily from US sources with extensive international coverage.

Features of each volume in the Global Viewpoints series include:

- An **annotated table of contents** that provides a brief summary of each essay in the volume, including the name of the country or area covered in the essay.

- An **introduction** specific to the volume topic.

- A **world map** to help readers locate the countries or areas covered in the essays.

- For each viewpoint, an **introduction** that contains notes about the author and source of the viewpoint explains why material from the specific country is being presented, summarizes the main points of the viewpoint, and offers three **guided reading questions** to aid in understanding and comprehension.

- **For further discussion** questions that promote critical thinking by asking the reader to compare and contrast aspects of the viewpoints or draw conclusions about perspectives and arguments.

- A worldwide list of **organizations to contact** for readers seeking additional information.

- A **periodical bibliography** for each chapter and a **bibliography of books** on the volume topic to aid in further research.

- A comprehensive **subject index** to offer access to people, places, events, and subjects cited in the text, with the countries covered in the viewpoints highlighted.

Global Viewpoints is designed for a broad spectrum of readers who want to learn more about current events, history, political science, government, international relations, economics, environmental science, world cultures, and sociology—students doing research for class assignments or debates, teachers and faculty seeking to supplement course materials, and others wanting to understand current issues better. By presenting how people in various countries perceive the root causes, current consequences, and proposed solutions to worldwide challenges, Global Viewpoints volumes offer readers opportunities to enhance their global awareness and their knowledge of cultures worldwide.

Introduction

"Suicide is a tragic global public health problem. Worldwide, more people die from suicide than from all homicides and wars combined. There is an urgent need for coordinated and intensified global action to prevent this needless toll."

—Dr. Catherine Le Galès-Camus,
assistant director-general,
Noncommunicable Diseases
and Mental Health,
World Health Organization

In the late 2000s, the US economic system began to falter. The US banking system, stretched thin by questionable financial dealings and practices, slowed and began to crack. Compounding the crisis was the collapse of the American housing market, which peaked in 2006. As the prices of homes fell, many owners opted to go into foreclosure rather than pay more on a house than it was worth on the market. The foreclosure epidemic further deteriorated the strength of US banking institutions; not only were banks saddled with the bad loans, but the epidemic led to the plummet of securities tied to US real estate pricing. During 2007–2008, more than one hundred mortgage lenders went bankrupt. Even large financial institutions were affected: Lehman Brothers went bankrupt; Bear Stearns, Merrill Lynch, and Wachovia were sold; and American International Group (AIG) and Washington Mutual were bailed out by the federal government. The implications of such large, once powerful financial institutions in crisis were profound and far-reaching.

The crisis soon expanded from the housing market to other parts of the economy; as businesses closed, state and local government revenues fell, the stock market plummeted, and consumer spending plunged. The United States was in a serious, full-fledged economic downturn.

With the global interconnectivity of today's modern economy, the impact of the US economic problems reverberated in economies all over the world. Foreign institutions involved in intricate and aggressive deals with failing US banking companies were caught on the hook. Worries about US financial institutions, the precipitous drop in the US stock market, concern over bank solvency and credit availability, and a general investor and consumer panic led to large losses in global stock markets. A series of highly publicized bank failures occurred in Europe. Like in the United States, world political leaders stepped in to offer bailout packages to avoid a complete collapse into global depression. Despite the coordinated efforts of political leaders, national ministers of finance, and central bank directors, by the end of October 2008 there was a currency crisis in Europe, forcing many politicians to request aid from the International Monetary Fund.

Developing countries were also hit hard by the economic downturn. Many of these countries relied on US spending and consumption; with the United States in recession and its spending down, economic growth in these countries slowed significantly. As a result, there has been a dramatic rise in the number of households living below the poverty line in countries such as Bangladesh and Ghana.

One of the unfortunate consequences of the global economic downturn was a sharp increase in suicide rates. In America, for example, there was a disturbing rise in suicide deaths in US communities that went into recession as early as 2005. Medical and law enforcement officials in these areas reported that it was undeniable that the stress of living with high rates of unemployment, home foreclosures, economic instability, and other factors associated with the recession had profoundly affected families and individuals. "We've had many situations where people lost their jobs and that was the reason for why they do what they do," said Sheriff Mark A. Hackel of Macomb County, Michigan, as reported on MSNBC.com. From 1979 to 2006, Macomb County had an average of eighty-one people committing suicide each year, according to the federal Centers for Disease Control and Prevention. In 2008, pounded by the collapse of the auto industry and an unemployment rate hovering around 18 percent, the number of suicides jumped to 178 in the first seven months of 2009. Another staggering sign that the recession caused a spike in the suicide rate in the United States was that the National Suicide Prevention Lifeline has reported a startling increase in the number of calls, from 13,423 calls in January 2007 to a high of 57,625 calls in August 2009.

With the economic downturn came stories of individuals devastated by professional or personal bankruptcy or foreclosure. Losing a lucrative and fulfilling job was also cited as a reason for high rates of depression and suicides. Yet the global recession also placed other stresses on individuals and families. Several studies show that the frequency and intensity of domestic violence rise dramatically in areas and times of economic instability; furthermore, there is a known link between domestic violence and both murder and suicides. Drug and alcohol abuse also factor into the problem. Long stints of unemployment can lead to social isolation, fragmentation and low social cohesion, all of which have long been identified as suicide factors.

Some analysts, however, assert that the reasons for taking one's own life are complicated, and can't be attributed to a single factor. They also maintain that there is no clear, established link between suicide rates and recent national recessions—only proven links between suicide and circumstances such as unemployment and home foreclosures that often result from a recession. One study shows that people who've lost their jobs commit suicide two to four times higher than those who are employed.

It is clear, however, that the global economic crisis has made it more difficult for those affected by depression and desperation to find help. Many mental health and suicide prevention programs worldwide lack funding in communities struggling with slashed budgets and declining revenues. In many situations, the communities that need these programs most cannot afford them.

The authors of the viewpoints presented in *Global Viewpoints: Suicide* discuss suicide trends worldwide including the deleterious effect the global economic downturn has had on some communities and provide an overview of several political, economic, and cultural factors that contribute to suicide rates. They also examine what national and local governments are doing to address suicide in their regions and survey suicide prevention efforts. The book concludes with a look at suicide as a form of terrorism, focusing on the increasing use of suicide bombing in recent years as a tool of terrorist groups.

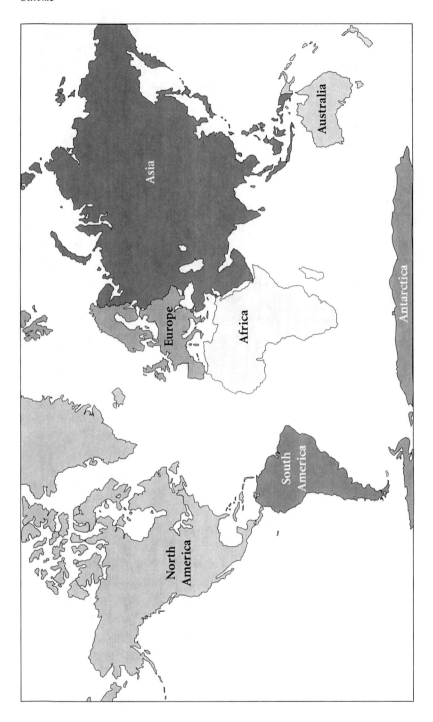

CHAPTER 1

Global Suicide Trends

Global Suicide Rates: An Overview

Organisation for Economic Co-operation and Development

The Organisation for Economic Co-operation and Development (OECD) is an international economic organization that works to stimulate trade and economic growth. In the following viewpoint, it identifies suicide as a major cause of death in many of its member countries. The OECD cites various factors that affect the suicide rate in individual countries, including age, economic conditions, and the efficacy of suicide prevention programs, and it underscores the importance of early detection and effective support and treatment to curb suicide.

As you read, consider the following questions:

1. According to the viewpoint, how many suicides were there in OECD countries in 2006?
2. What countries had the fewest suicides, according to the OECD?
3. What OECD countries had the most?

The intentional killing of oneself is evidence not only of personal breakdown, but also of a deterioration of the social context in which an individual lives. Suicide may be the end point of a number of different contributing factors. It is

Organisation for Economic Co-operation and Development, "Suicide," *Health at a Glance 2009: OECD Indicators*, OECD Publishing, 2009. www.dx.doi.org. Copyright © 2009 by OECD. All rights reserved. Reproduced by permission.

more likely to occur during crisis periods associated with divorce, alcohol and drug abuse, unemployment, clinical depression and other forms of mental illness. Because of this, suicide is often used as a proxy indicator of the mental health status of a population. However, the number of suicides in certain countries may be underestimated because of the stigma that is associated with the act, or because of data issues associated with reporting criteria.

Suicide is a significant cause of death in many OECD [Organisation for Economic Co-operation and Development] countries, and there were 140,000 such deaths in 2006. In 2006, there were fewest suicides in southern European countries (Greece, Italy and Spain) and in Mexico and the United Kingdom, at less than seven deaths per 100,000 population. They were highest in Korea, Hungary, Japan and Finland, at 18 or more deaths per 100,000 population. There is more than a sevenfold difference between Korea and Greece, the countries with the lowest and highest death rates.

Suicides Are Decreasing in Many Countries

Since 1990, suicide rates have decreased in many OECD countries, with pronounced declines of 40% or more in Denmark, Luxembourg and Hungary. Despite this progress, Hungary still has one of the highest rates among OECD countries. On the other hand, death rates from suicides have increased the most since 1990 in Korea, Mexico and Japan, although in Mexico rates remain at low levels. In Korea and Japan, suicide rates now stand well above the OECD average. Korea almost tripled from 12 per 100,000 in 1990 to 32 in 2006, and suicide rates among women are the highest among OECD countries, at 13 per 100,000. Economic downturn, weakening social integration and the erosion of the traditional family support base for the elderly have all been implicated in Korea's recent increase in suicide rates.

World Suicide Rates by Country, 2005

Country	Suicide Rates per 100,000 People
Austria	13.8
Belgium	18.4
Britain	6.0
Canada	10.2
Czech Republic	12.7
Denmark	11.3
Finland	16.5
France	14.6
Germany	10.3
Greece	2.9
Hungary	21.0
Iceland	10.4
Italy	5.5
Japan	19.4
Luxembourg	9.5
Mexico	4.4
Netherlands	7.9
New Zealand	11.9
Norway	10.9
Poland	13.8
Portugal	8.7
Slovak Republic	10.9
South Korea	24.7
Spain	6.3
Sweden	11.1
United States	10.1

TAKEN FROM: Organisation for Economic Cooperation and Development.

In general, death rates from suicides are three to four times greater for men than for women across OECD countries, and this gender gap has been fairly stable over time. The gender gap is narrower for attempted suicides, reflecting the fact that women tend to use less fatal methods than men.

Suicide is also related to age, with young people aged under 25 and elderly people especially at risk. While suicide rates among the latter have generally declined over the past two decades, almost no progress has been observed among younger people.

In general, death rates from suicides are three to four times greater for men than for women across OECD countries, and this gender gap has been fairly stable over time.

Since suicides are, in the vast majority of cases, linked with depression and alcohol and other substance abuse, the early detection of these psychosocial problems in high-risk groups by families, social workers and health professionals must be part of suicide-prevention campaigns, together with the provision of effective support and treatment. With suicide receiving increasing attention worldwide, many countries are promoting mental health and developing national strategies for prevention, focussing on at-risk groups.

South Korea Is Plagued by the Highest Suicide Rate in the Industrialized World

Blaine Harden

Blaine Harden is a reporter for the Washington Post. *In the following viewpoint, he notes that the suicide rate in South Korea is very high compared to other industrialized nations, with a particularly high rate in the rural elderly, educated South Koreans in their 20s and 30s, and celebrities. Harden attributes the exploding suicide rate in the country to stress brought on by the demands of modernity.*

As you read, consider the following questions:

1. How many South Koreans kill themselves each day, according to Harden?
2. According to the viewpoint, how much higher is the South Korean suicide rate than the American rate?
3. What does Harden claim is the leading cause of death among South Koreans in their 20s and 30s?

Choi Jin-young hanged himself last month with an electrical cord. The 39-year-old actor wasn't getting any work in local TV, police said, and he had been depressed since the suicide of his famous older sister.

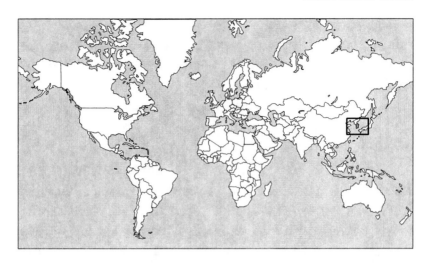

The sister, Choi Jin-sil, was known as the "nation's actress." When she hanged herself in her bathroom in October 2008, a wave of sympathetic suicides swept South Korea and 1,700 people took their lives the following month.

Seven months later, former president Roh Moo-hyun jumped off a cliff to his death. "I can't begin to fathom the countless agonies down the road," he wrote in a note. Then a 20-year-old Chanel model, Daul Kim, killed herself, posting a blog entry that said: "Mad depressed and overworked." Another said: "The more I gain, the more lonely it is."

And so it ends for 35 South Koreans a day. The suicide rate in this prosperous nation of about 50 million people has doubled in the past decade and is now the highest in the industrialized world.

The rate of suicide in most other wealthy countries peaked in the early 1980s, but the toll in South Korea continues to climb. Twenty-six people per 100,000 committed suicide in 2008 (the most recent year for which data are available). That's 2 1/2 times the rate in the United States and significantly higher than in nearby Japan, where suicide is deeply embedded in the culture.

Before South Korea got rich, wired and worried, its suicide rate was among the lowest in the industrialized world. But modernity has spawned inordinate levels of stress. People here work more, sleep less and spend more money per capita on cram schools than residents of the 29 other industrialized countries that belong to the Organisation for Economic Co-operation and Development.

Still, it remains a taboo here to admit to feeling over-whelmed by stress. The word "psychiatry" has such a negative connotation that many leading hospitals have created departments of "neuro-psychiatry," in the hope that people perceive care as medical treatment and not as a public admission of character failure.

Before he hanged himself last month, Choi Jin-young had been struggling with serious depression, his friends told reporters. But they said he refused to consider psychiatric treatment.

Before South Korea got rich, wired and worried, its suicide rate was among the lowest in the industrialized world.

"This is the dark aspect of our rapid development," said Ha Kyooseob, a psychiatrist at Seoul National University College of Medicine and head of the Korean Association for Suicide Prevention. "We are unwilling to seek help for depression. We are very afraid of being seen as crazy."

Denial extends to relatives of suicide victims. Recent attempts by the Ministry of Health and Welfare and suicide prevention groups to interview the families of those who kill themselves have produced little cooperation.

"When we go to the families and ask questions about why it happened, they say to us, 'Do not kill him twice,'" Ha said. "We have tried to interview hundreds of families, but we have

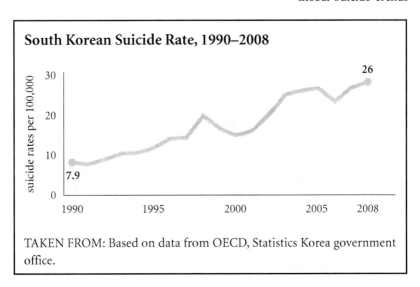

South Korean Suicide Rate, 1990–2008

TAKEN FROM: Based on data from OECD, Statistics Korea government office.

only been allowed to talk to a few of them. If one is dead from suicide, everything is a secret."

Incidents of suicide are increasing most rapidly among the rural elderly, government figures show, driven among other things by isolation, illness and poverty. Suicide among the young has been abetted by the long hours South Koreans spend online. Police investigators say the Internet enables young people to meet and plan group suicides, even when they are strangers to one another and live in different cities.

Suicide is the leading cause of death among South Koreans in their 20s and 30s, and it is the fourth leading cause of death overall, after cancer, stroke and heart disease.

Suicide among the young has been abetted by the long hours South Koreans spend online.

Yet what has particularly caught the eye of the public and the news media is a flurry of chain-reaction suicides among the rich and famous.

Choi Jin-young's suicide generated front-page headlines, reminding the public of the suicide of his beloved sister, who killed herself after becoming distressed over Internet rumors that linked her to the suicide of another celebrity, comedian Ahn Jae-hwan.

No studies have found a statistically significant increase in suicide among the nation's elite. Still, noisy news coverage of these deaths has caught the public's imagination, and that worries Ha, the psychiatrist.

Government data show that suicides can trigger copycat behavior. Choi Jin-sil's death triggered a 70 percent increase in the suicide rate. It lasted for about a month, resulting in 700 more deaths during that time than would normally be expected.

"Famous suicides have a really bad influence," Ha said.

Egypt Is Alarmed by Its Rising Suicide Rate

Jano Charbel

Jano Charbel is a contributor to Al-Masry Al-Youm. *In the following viewpoint, Charbel observes that there has been a significant increase in the number of suicides in Egypt since 1987, but contends that precise statistics are not kept because moral and religious stigmas prevent many families from reporting the incident to the proper authorities. Charbel explains that suicides are covered up by the media and government officials and reports that Arab officials admit that suicides and suicide attempts throughout the Arab world have been underreported for years.*

As you read, consider the following questions:

1. According to estimates by the World Health Organization, what will be the global annual suicide rate by 2020?
2. How many suicides are estimated in Egypt per year, according to the viewpoint?
3. According to 1987 estimates, how many Egyptians committed suicide that year?

September 10 is World Suicide Prevention Day, a day not widely celebrated or even known about, which reflects the uphill struggle faced by those trying to promote the aims of the campaign.

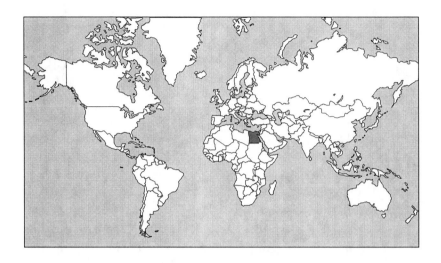

According to statistics compiled by the UN's World Health Organization (WHO), every year approximately one million people worldwide commit suicide—almost one death every 40 seconds. Suicide rates are reported to be rising steadily in developing countries, primarily amongst those between the ages of 15 and 44. WHO reports that for every death there are around 20 other people who will have attempted suicide. Its projections indicate that the number of suicides may rise to 1.5 million annually by the year 2020.

According to undefined estimates provided by WHO's Suicide Prevention program, Japan, Russia, Ukraine, South Korea, and much of northern Europe reported suicide rates of over 13 per 100,000 people. The former Soviet republics of Lithuania, Belarus, and Kazakhstan reported the world's highest reported suicide rates. Jordan reportedly has the lowest rate of suicide in the Arab world, and one of the lowest worldwide.

Figuring Egypt's Suicide Rate

As for Egypt, it is reported to have an annual suicide rate of less than 6.5 per 100,000—or fewer than 5070 deaths by suicide each year. Exactly how many Egyptians do commit suicide each year? Estimates are available, but there are no definitive statistics.

According to a report published in a leading state-owned newspaper (June 2010) which cited numbers issued by a government body, the Central Agency for Public Mobilization and Statistics, a total of 1160 suicides were reported in the year 2005, followed by 2355 in 2006, with the number rising to 3700 in 2007. In 2008 approximately 4000 Egyptians took their own lives, while 50,000 attempted suicides were reported in the same year. In 2009 an estimated 5000 Egyptians killed themselves—and another 104,000 suicide attempts were reported. The report does not include a breakdown of the numbers by age or gender.

These statistics are particularly shocking in comparison to those issued by the Egyptian state in 1987. Only a quarter of a century ago, Egypt officially registered an annual suicide rate of 0.1 out of 100,000—all males: No females reportedly took their own lives. According to the demographics of that time, this translates to around just 24 deaths through suicide each year.

Exactly how many Egyptians do commit suicide each year? Estimates are available, but there are no definitive statistics.

Doctors Confirm the Increase

Commenting on these numbers, Dr. Mohamed Rakha, a psychiatric physician at Abbasiya Hospital for Mental Illness said these statistics are plausible. He explained that psychiatric doctors have noted an increased rate of suicides. "Medical studies indicate a definite increase in the number of people contemplating suicide over the past few years, and we are personally dealing with more people who have attempted suicide. But we are a long way from having a complete picture of Egypt's suicide problem."

According to Rakha, there are no precise statistics available because many cases of suicide are not officially documented.

What the Qur'an Says About Suicide

Destroy not yourselves. Surely Allah is ever merciful to you.

Qur'an 4:29

The Prophet said: "Amongst the nations before you there was a man who got a wound, and growing impatient (with its pain), he took a knife and cut his hand with it and the blood did not stop till he died. Allah said, 'My Slave hurried to bring death upon himself so I have forbidden him (to enter) Paradise.'"

Sahih Bukhari 4.56.669

BBC, "Euthanasia and Suicide," September 7, 2009.

"Very often families of suicide victims seek to cover up, or to avoid mentioning that a family member has taken their own life." He added that there are serious moral and religious stigmas involved: "Families do not want people to remember that their son or daughter died as a so-called apostate. Covering up a suicide is often perceived as the only way to preserve the reputation of the deceased, and the reputation of the family."

Reasons for Increase

Rakha says that "more than ten percent of those suffering from depression contemplate suicide, in one way or another." But it's not only depression that spurs people into committing suicide. There are a number of other mental health problems which could prompt thoughts of suicide, such as schizophrenia—which may manifest itself as self-destructive voices heard in one's mind telling the sufferer to harm or kill themselves. "Other mental conditions that, if left untreated, may lead to suicide include obsessive-compulsive disorder, alcoholism, and drug addiction. These psychological problems may lead to chemical imbalances, panic attacks, behavioral disturbances, and reckless driving—all of which may lead to intentional or unintentional death."

According to Rakha, most deaths by suicide are typically preceded by several failed attempts. He also argues that weaker societal bonds, along with pressures of all sorts—whether educational, political, social, financial, professional, familial, personal and/or emotional—may lead people to contemplate suicide.

Suicides have been reported amongst Christians and Muslims, singles and married people, teachers and students, the employed and those without work, staff and bosses.

Rates in Islamic Countries

A WHO news bulletin entitled "Choosing to Die—A Growing Epidemic Among the Young" says that Islamic countries tend to have some of the lowest suicide rates in the world, and while the figures may sometimes be low because death certificates avoid mentioning suicide, some researchers believe they are largely genuine. According to WHO, Iran, for example, had 0.3 suicides per 100,000 men and 0.1 per 100,000 women in 1991, the latest year for which figures are available.

An official from the Ministry of Health [and Medical Education], who withheld his name because he is not authorized to speak to the media, told *Al-Masry Al-Youm*, "The data pertaining to the annual numbers of suicides cannot be verified. There are numerous reasons—religious, cultural, and societal—why information about suicides is kept hidden." The official went on to say, "Suicides and suicide attempts throughout the Arab world are underreported. The statistics available do not reflect the reality or the magnitude of this massive problem."

The "Village Suicides"

Filmmaker Maggie Morgan examined this issue in her 2009 documentary *Village Suicides*. Her field study and film revolves around Mair, a predominantly Coptic village near the city of Assiut, in Upper Egypt. In this marginalized village with a population of 10,000, Morgan documented 45 deaths by suicide during the year 2008 alone. According to the filmmaker, "There are hardly any jobs in Mair. There is no industry, no entertainment, and an extremely rigid structure of social, religious, and familial control." Numerous villagers attempt to escape these confines and travel abroad for work or immigration—generally either to the Arab Gulf or the United States.

Those who find themselves unable to leave have frequently resorted to ending their lives by swallowing a pill—intended for use as an agricultural insecticide. "The poison is extremely lethal and fast acting. One pill can kill in less than half an hour." Morgan added that authorities recently moved to ban the sale of this insecticide, in its tablet form, when it was discovered that people were using it to commit suicide.

Cases of suicide, and suicide attempts, are increasingly covered in local newspapers. Suicides have been reported amongst Christians and Muslim, singles and married people, teachers and students, the employed and those without work, staff and bosses. An international press report mentioned that Egypt's national center for toxins has registered approximately 2700 attempted suicides committed by single women in 2009 alone.

Japan's Youth Suicide Rate Is Fueled by Internet Suicide Pacts

David McNeill

David McNeill is a reporter for the Independent. *In the following viewpoint, he describes the recent tragic trend of young suicidal Japanese men and women meeting up on the Internet to form suicide pacts. McNeill observes that although the trend has forced Internet providers to monitor cyberspace and police to focus on Internet communications, mental health experts argue that the focus should be on treating the root problems that spur individuals to consider suicide.*

As you read, consider the following questions:

1. According to the viewpoint, how many people in Japan committed suicide together after meeting via the web in 2005?

2. How many people per day took their own lives in Japan in 2003?

3. What is the current suicide rate in Japan, according to McNeill?

Young Japanese people are still joining group-suicide pacts in record numbers despite efforts to crack down on the bizarre Internet-led phenomenon.

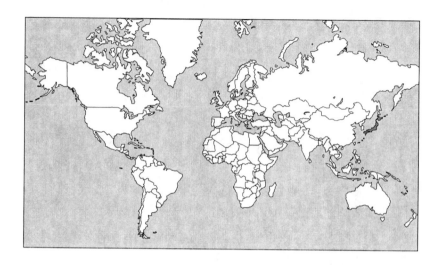

Japanese police said yesterday [February 9, 2006] that a record 91 people had committed suicide together after meeting via the web in 2005, up from 55 people the previous year. The figure has tripled since the police began keeping records in 2003. Most of the victims were in their teens, twenties and thirties and sought each other out via websites that allow the suicidal to swap e-mail addresses, share stories and offer advice on the surest, least painful ways to die.

Many opt for carbon monoxide poisoning in sealed vehicles, often in secluded or scenic areas, like four young men who died while watching the sun rise from a car at the foot of Mount Fuji. The men met for the first time just hours before their death.

Addressing the Problem

The latest statistics will likely lead to more demands for monitoring of cyberspace, including renewed calls to ban the word "suicide" from search engines. Net service providers already work with the police and there are signs the group-suicide phenomenon may have peaked. But Yukio Saito, who runs Japan's largest telephone helpline, cautions against complacency. "People will always find a way to end their lives if they want to. The wider issues must be tackled."

In Japan, 94 people took their own lives every day in 2003, setting a record of 34,427 that broke the previous high of 33,048, in 1999. Since the Asian crash of 1997–8, when the statistics jumped 35 per cent, suicides have claimed more than 220,000 lives, approximately the population of Derby [in the United Kingdom]. A suicide manual that lists effective ways of ending it all—including hanging, electrocution and pills—has sold more than a million copies. In true Japanese style it rates these methods in terms of the pain and trouble they cause to others; predictably, jumping in front of a train is given a maximum rating of five.

Dozens of young Japanese can be found every day discussing suicide on online chat rooms.

Better Mental Healthcare Needed

The dramatic rise in suicides forced the health ministry to bring out a package of proposals at the end of 2002, including a drastic boost in mental healthcare facilities. But Japan still has far fewer psychiatrists than other advanced countries, and family doctors routinely misdiagnose mental illness. A health ministry survey found that more than half of the workers recognised as having committed suicide due to work-related stress between 1999 and 2002 had been working at least 100 hours overtime a month. "This is a suicide epidemic," says Mr Saito. "We are not doing enough to help people who are suffering in silence."

Japan is not unique. South Korea has also experienced a wave of suicide pacts, and Ireland has seen a 45 per cent increase in suicides over the past decade. But, at 24.1 per 100,000 people, Japan has the highest per-capita suicide rate in the developed world. Nearly 8,000 people in their twenties and thirties killed themselves in 2003, making suicide one of the leading causes of death for young Japanese. Many of these youngsters are drawn from the ranks of *hikikomori*, social recluses who have locked themselves in their rooms, sometimes for years on end.

Cultural Factors

Many are linked to the outside world only through the electronic umbilical cord of their computers, which they use to find like-minded folk. Dozens of young Japanese can be found every day discussing suicide on online chat rooms. A typical message reads: "If you are thinking about killing yourself, please reply." Another says: "I'm in my early twenties and I want to die easily. I can go anywhere in Japan." Fittingly, perhaps, one of the last acts of the suicidal is often to e-mail a friend or relative. Several times in the past two years the police have stumbled on semi-asphyxiated young people just in time, after similar messages were sent.

Japan Is Falsely Stereotyped as the "Suicide Nation"

Kris Kosaka

Kris Kosaka is a contributor to the Japan Times. *In the following viewpoint, Kosaka argues that the stereotype of Japan as the "suicide nation" has hampered endeavors to fully and effectively address the root problems that cause suicide attempts. Kosaka contends that the myth that Japan is a suicide culture is perpetuated by both Japanese and Western media and should be finally put to rest.*

As you read, consider the following questions:

1. According to the author, how has Western media reinforced the idea of Japan as a "suicide nation"?
2. How, according to the author, does Japanese media perpetuate the myth of Japan as a "suicide nation"?
3. What does the author see as a more practical reason for Japan's high suicide rate?

Now that spring has dissolved into the sticky humidity of rainy season, now that *go gatsu byo*—"May sickness"— has melted away along with the memory of the cherry blossoms, perhaps it is time to wash away one of the most pervasive stereotypes of Japan, its dubious status as a "suicide nation."

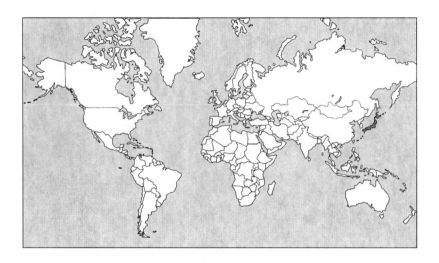

Western media endlessly speculates and blames: Last year [2008] the *Economist* cited Japan's unforgiving society and "samurai traditions," while the *Observer* detailed Japan's "grim reputation" as a suicide nation while highlighting the trend of online suicide pacts. True, Japan's rates remain among the highest in the world for industrialized countries, yet, depression, ennui, hopelessness—all are universal emotions every human faces at one point or another. To assume Japanese people have a pronounced proclivity toward "jisatsu" neatly plays into several untrue stereotypes of Japanese culture.

Japanese Stereotypes

One stereotype concerns samurai and seppuku. In recent history, the use of kamikaze pilots or *nikudan* (human bullets) cemented Japan's reputation for condoning suicide. Personal letters and testimonies left behind, however, prove that the pilots' sacrifice was not always voluntary and that they were certainly not the willing martyrs widely assumed.

Both legendary and modern figures of Japanese history have committed suicide, but not significantly more than in other countries. Contrary to popular belief, Japanese executives do not sacrifice it all to take responsibility for a company's problems. Yet stereotype once again appeared in the international news recently when U.S. Senator Charles Grassley suggested AIG [American International Group] executives follow "the Japanese example" and take a bow of apology and then resign or commit suicide. (Grassley later amended his statement, saying he "obviously" didn't mean they should really kill themselves.)

While every summer in Japan brings ghost stories, every spring—as it conjures mortality with the ephemeral cherry blossoms—invariably calls forth stories of self-slaughter. News reports feature the suicide rate (this year, with the financial crisis, they required a monthly breakdown). Famous suicide sites throughout Japan become newsworthy again, and articles appear discussing "suicide culture."

Another, more practical reason for the high suicide rate is the graying of Japan.

How the Myth Is Perpetuated

In this way, suicide pervades Japanese society more openly than in other cultures, where it is considered a mortal sin and discussion of the subject is generally avoided. The myth of Japan as a suicide nation is surely fed by the Japanese media and many people on the streets. If a train delays, it's not unusual for my Japanese friends to jest that it must be the season: not winter, spring, summer or autumn, but the season of platform suicides. As much as Western media broadcasts this social problem, nothing beats the coverage here in Japan.

Another, more practical reason for the high suicide rate is the graying of Japan. Worldwide, suicides occur more often in the elderly, and Japan has more elderly than most countries.

A Final Stereotype

A final, pervasive stereotype is found in the media: the cold, unforgiving Japanese society. This stereotype particularly insults the Japanese. Each society, by its very definition, contains a straitjacket of norms and unspoken rules for behavior. Most of us traverse an entire existence unaware of these invisible binds surrounding us, especially if residing in our native culture throughout our lives.

To imply that Japanese individuals are abnormally vicious or unforgiving implies they are less than human. Certainly, Japanese society is not perfect, but no society is without flaws and strictures. A necessary part of any human's growth is learning to balance society's demands and individual's needs.

End the Myth

Knowing the reality of the Japanese mentality and societal workings, government and media should work together on the reasons leading to suicide, not help sensationalize the aftermath. Life is sacred and precious; life is pain and suffering. If one lives long enough, one will experience both ends of the spectrum. For anyone, suicide lurks under the rising sun each morning, and to assume Japanese are particularly susceptible refutes the many with a *ganbatte*—"never-say-die"—spirit.

If only the media, both inside and out of the country, would stop promoting the stereotype of Japan, perhaps the underlying issues could be addressed: financial distress; depression in the elderly or ill; copycat or trend suicides; bullying or apathy among the young.

Knowing the reality of the Japanese mentality and societal workings, government and media should work together on the reasons leading to suicide, not help sensationalize the aftermath.

If spring is a season of contradictions in Japan, one of both rebirth and transience, the persistent "plum rains" (*tsuyu*) of June call to mind the stubborn tang of life amid the gloom.

Enough pointing fingers at Japan for its darkness alone: Across the world, we are all humans, with vulnerabilities, flaws and redeeming strengths.

Australia's Suicide Rate Is Higher than Initially Reported

Ruth Pollard

Ruth Pollard is an investigative reporter for the Sydney Morning Herald. *In the following viewpoint, she asserts that the Australian government statistics on suicide have been severely underreported, casting doubt on the official report that the suicide rate has significantly dropped since the 1990s. Pollard observes that revised statistics reveal that the suicide toll in Australia remains about the same, with experts predicting a rising rate of suicide attributed to the economic downturn.*

As you read, consider the following questions:

1. According to the NSW Clinical Excellence Commission, how many people died from suicide within seven days of contact with the health system from December 2006 to June 2008?

2. What does John Mendoza believe the real Australian rate of suicide is?

3. What is the official suicide rate in Australia according to the Australian Bureau of Statistics?

A ustralia has dangerously miscalculated its suicide statistics—by as much as 30 per cent in NSW and Queensland—leaving a silent and growing epidemic of mounting deaths.

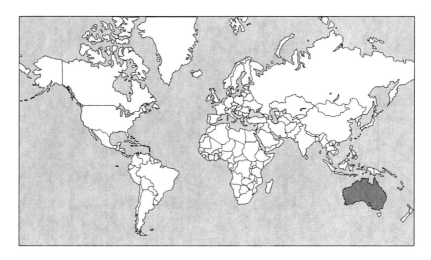

The figures are in stark contrast to years of backslapping by state and federal governments, congratulating themselves for reducing suicide rates from a peak of 2700 in 1997.

The *Herald* can reveal the suicide toll is as high now as it was in the 1990s—if not higher—with experts predicting a further rise as the impact of rising unemployment and other economic factors bite.

The dangerous combination of government underinvestment, shutting families out of hospital and police processes, a lack of training and a general community malaise about how to prevent suicide means so many are falling through the cracks.

Ten people each month take their lives either inside a state health facility or within a week of having contact with one.

Discharged too soon from emergency departments, left unobserved in psychiatric wards or denied admission to overcrowded inpatient facilities, their deaths reveal a pattern of repeated systemic failures that demands urgent reform.

The dangerous combination of government underinvestment, shutting families out of hospital and police processes, a

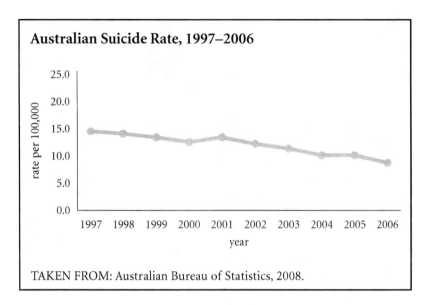

Australian Suicide Rate, 1997–2006

TAKEN FROM: Australian Bureau of Statistics, 2008.

lack of training and a general community malaise about how to prevent suicide means so many are falling through the cracks.

In the 18 months to June 2008, at least 175 people died from suicide within seven days of contact with the health system, figures from the NSW Clinical Excellence Commission show.

A coroner's inquest into a man who shot himself within hours of being discharged from hospital concluded last week, with police and health departments questioned over their protocols for dealing with people at risk.

In another death, in which a woman set fire to herself after being denied help by a public hospital, the coroner noted: "This death was preventable and is probably the most tragic example of NSW Health's inability and/or failure to deal with individual cases in an appropriate manner."

John Mendoza, an adjunct associate professor at the University of Sydney faculty of medicine, said the real rate of suicide was about 2500–2700. "With this economic downturn we can expect that to increase by around 10 per cent, so we are looking at approximately 3000 people each year," he said. "None of this takes into account suicides by way of single vehicle accidents—these are the only aspect of road accident deaths rising as a percentage of total deaths."

These figures indicate a major health problem and are much higher than the Bureau of Statistics count of 1800 suicide deaths a year, said Professor Mendoza, who is chairman of the Federal Government's National Advisory Council on Mental Health.

"It is a hidden epidemic and yet the Federal Government only invests $1 per person per year on suicide prevention."

The director of health and vital statistics at the Australian Bureau of Statistics, Tara Pritchard, confirmed the bureau would release updated figures in March to correct the undercounting.

"What that revision of ABS data will show us is that really we have gone nowhere in terms of overall reductions from the peaks in suicide rates in the early 1990s, and we have certainly gone nowhere among reducing suicide in indigenous populations. They remain four times higher overall," Professor Mendoza said.

Governments had done little more than the bare minimum to prevent deaths, said Dawn O'Neil, chief executive officer of Lifeline.

"Once we got confirmation the rates were not coming down . . . the Government didn't want to know, politically they wanted to believe that the suicide rates were falling."

China's Female Suicide Crisis Is Waning

Megan Shank

Megan Shank is a writer and translator. In the following viewpoint, she reports that an alarming number of rural Chinese women have killed themselves using a common toxic pesticide banned in many countries. Shank notes that new regulations have limited and even banned the use of some of these products and recent evidence shows that China's female suicide epidemic is waning.

As you read, consider the following questions:

1. According to the World Health Organization, pesticide ingestion is involved in what percentage of Chinese suicides?

2. According to the viewpoint, what percentage of Chinese suicide survivors thought about suicide for just five minutes before attempted suicide?

3. According to a 2008 study, how much has the Chinese suicide rate declined over the past two decades?

In many rural Chinese homes, a jar of pesticide—often a variety banned in Western countries—sits in the family outhouse. Even after harvest, farmers are loath to throw out the

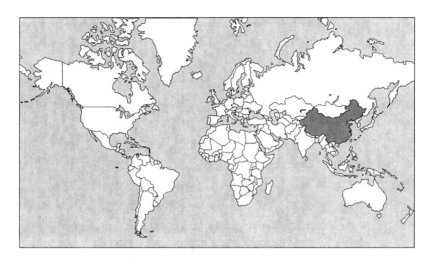

remainder. Despite Chinese President Hu Jintao's promise to create a "harmonious society" by improving people's livelihood and reducing the gap between wealthy cities and the impoverished countryside, surviving in China's rural areas still requires thrift.

But the pesticide that ensures an abundant crop all too often reaps sorrow.

Pesticide ingestion is involved in 60 percent of Chinese suicides, according to the World Health Organization, which published a 2009 report suggesting a link between exposure to organophosphate pesticides, the type commonly used in China, and suicidal thoughts.

Rural Chinese women—with their easy access to toxic pesticides, social isolation, and unique burden of feudal obligations and modern stresses—have been particularly susceptible.

A widely reported March 2002 study in the British medical journal *The Lancet*, by Michael Phillips, executive director of the WHO suicide prevention center in Beijing, reported that from 1995 to 1999, suicide was the No. 1 cause of death for Chinese young adults aged 15 to 34. Rural suicide rates were three times higher than urban rates, and women had a

25 percent higher suicide rate than men—making China one of the few nations with that distinction.

Worldwide, female suicide attempts outnumber men's three to one, but men have higher rates of suicide death. In China, though, women have experienced a higher rate of finished suicide attempts because they use a more effective method: pesticide. "In the West, you take a couple Valium, you get taken to the ER and washed out, and you go home," Phillips told *The Daily Beast.* "In China, you take half a cup of pesticide and you're dead two hours later."

Rural Chinese women—with their easy access to toxic pesticides, social isolation, and unique burden of feudal obligations and modern stresses—have been particularly susceptible.

After the release of Phillips' 2002 report, China's atypical suicide gender gap garnered headlines around the world. The Western and Chinese media breathlessly spun the tale of Chinese college grads unable to find jobs and seeking solace in suicide—unsubstantiated press fodder, according to Phillips, since the real problem was the country's poorest and most vulnerable women.

Chinese women pride themselves on their ability to "eat bitterness," or put up with sadness and stress. But every woman has her breaking point. In the West, 90 percent of all suicidal behavior occurs in individuals with long-term mental illness. But 40 percent of Chinese suicide survivors thought about suicide for just five minutes before they acted; 60 percent considered it for less than two hours. And once the deed is done, many country doctors are ill-equipped to manage pesticide poisoning.

There's evidence though, that China's female suicide crisis is waning. A 2008 study by Phillips reported a 57 percent decline in Chinese suicides over the past two decades—largely

The Drop in China's Suicide Rate

Jing Jun, a professor of sociology in Tsinghua University, and his students took one year to set up the first national database on suicide rate to grasp the overall trend of suicides in China. . . .

Jing has found that one of the main reasons why the suicide rate has dropped was the steady and big decline in the number of suicides committed by rural women. The suicide rate among rural women declined sharply from 0.03 percent in 1987 to less than 0.01 percent in 2009.

Wang Yiqing, "Who Says Suicide Rate Is Rising?"
China Daily, *November 11, 2010.*

due to decreased death among rural women. Experts attribute this change to a decrease in pesticide access. For years, the WHO has called on China to ban the most toxic pesticides. In 2008, the Ministry of Agriculture released new regulations on pesticides, including legislation to phase some out of use, though it is unclear how well this can be enforced. In the meantime, Phillips' Beijing center has installed 10,000 lock-boxes for pesticide storage in Shaanxi Province in order to decrease access to the poisonous substance; a similar program in Sri Lanka has shown favorable preliminary results. And as more Chinese women abandon farmwork for opportunities in the city, they are also further removed from pesticide's deadly call.

Declining suicide rates among rural women are also likely the result of enhanced social networks and increased economic and social emancipation. Because suicide in China is the result of impulsive action rather than long-term depression, women's health advocates emphasize that isolated women require social support, not just SSRIs. Traditionally, when a rural woman marries, she leaves her hometown, her family, and her friends to live with her husband's family, which creates a gender imbalance and isolates the women, says Xu Rong, head of the Suicide Prevention Project with the Beijing Cultural Development Center for Rural Women.

When a couple has problems, the husband's family will usually take his side, even if he is abusing her, says Xie Lihua, founding editor of *Rural Women* magazine. Xie estimates more than 70 percent of rural suicidal behavior is the result of domestic strife. The notion that the home is an intensely private place prevents women from seeking outside help.

China's social and economic modernization have given rural women more access to education, technology, jobs, and divorce, but critics say national and local governments must be more proactive in fighting suicide.

Women ingest pesticide in a moment of crisis because they have no emotional outlet or empathetic support, says Xu, whose organization set up support groups for rural women in northeastern China. In a moment of blinding rage over a cheating husband, a bad crop, or a critical mother-in-law, when a woman wants to end it all, having a place to talk over roiling emotions with other women and brainstorm positive problem-solving strategies can mean the difference between life and death.

China's social and economic modernization have given rural women more access to education, technology, jobs, and divorce, but critics say national and local governments must be more proactive in fighting suicide. China has failed to produce a national suicide prevention plan and local governments focus almost exclusively on GDP growth, says Zhang Chun, director of the Nanjing Psychological Crisis Center.

"When I was putting together the center in 2004, a local official warned me not to turn Nanjing into a tragic city because it would negatively impact the investment climate," he recalls. Zhang estimates his center fields 2,700 crisis calls a year—80 percent are from women—yet he receives little government funding. "The government needs to pay more attention to people's livelihood," he says, "to allow people to live with dignity."

India Is Experiencing an Epidemic of Farmer Suicides

Vandana Shiva

Vandana Shiva is an environmental activist and the founder and director of Navdanya, a program of the Research Foundation for Science, Technology, and Ecology. In the following viewpoint, she reports that there has been a marked increase in the number of suicides of cotton farmers across four Indian states: Punjab, Karnataka, Maharashtra, and Andhra Pradesh. Shiva attributes the rise of suicides to the trend of corporate seed producers establishing seed monopolies, which lead to less profits, increased debt, and more economic pressures on Indian farmers in these areas.

As you read, consider the following questions:

1. How many cotton farmers have committed suicide in India since 1997, according to the author?
2. According to the viewpoint, in which district did the farmers' suicides start?
3. In the Vidarbha region of Maharashtra, how has the area under Bt cotton increased from 2004 to 2007?

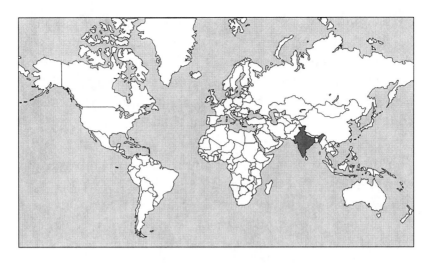

An epidemic of farmers' suicides has spread across four Indian states—Maharashtra, Andhra Pradesh, Karnataka, and Punjab—over the last decade. According to official data, more than 160,000 farmers have committed suicide in India since 1997.

The Impact of Seed Companies

These suicides are most frequent where farmers grow cotton, and appear directly linked to the presence of seed monopolies. For the supply of cotton seeds in India has increasingly slipped out of the hands of farmers and into the hands of global seed producers like Monsanto. These giant corporations have begun to control local seed companies through buyouts, joint ventures, and licensing arrangements, leading to seed monopolies.

When this happens, seed is transformed from being a common good into being the "intellectual property" of companies such as Monsanto, for which the corporation can claim limitless profits through royalty payments. For farmers, this means deeper debt.

Seed is also transformed in this way from being a renewable regenerative resource into a nonrenewable resource and commodity. Seed scarcity is directly caused by seed monopolies, which have as their ultimate weapon a "terminator" seed that is engineered for sterility. This means that farmers can't renew their own supply but must return to the monopolist for new seed each planting season. For farmers, this means higher costs; for seed corporations, higher profits.

The creation of seed monopolies is based on the deregulation of seed corporations, including giving them oversight over biosafety. With the coming of globalization, seed companies were allowed to sell seeds for which the companies had certified their safety. In the case of genetically engineered seed, these companies are again seeking self-regulation for biosafety.

The creation of seed monopolies, and with them crushing debts to a new species of moneylender—the agents of the seed and chemical companies—has taken a high human toll as well.

The Human Toll

State regulation does continue to exist where seeds are concerned, but nowadays it is aimed at farmers, who are being pushed into dependency on patented, corporate seed. Such compulsory licensing is a big cause of the global destruction of biodiversity. The creation of seed monopolies, and with them crushing debts to a new species of moneylender—the agents of the seed and chemical companies—has taken a high human toll as well.

The farm suicides first started in the district of Warangal in Andhra Pradesh. Peasants in Warangal used to grow millets, pulses, and oilseeds. Overnight, Warangal was converted to a cotton-growing district based on nonrenewable hybrids that require irrigation and are prone to pest attacks. Small peasants without capital were trapped in a vicious cycle of debt. Some saw only one way out.

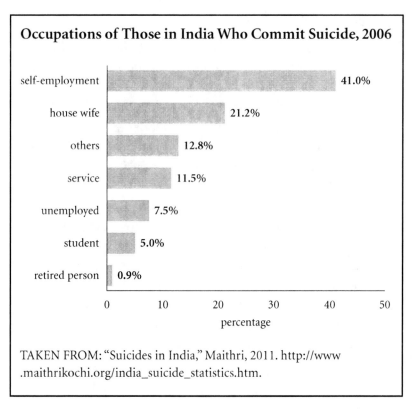

Occupations of Those in India Who Commit Suicide, 2006

Occupation	Percentage
self-employment	41.0%
house wife	21.2%
others	12.8%
service	11.5%
unemployed	7.5%
student	5.0%
retired person	0.9%

percentage

TAKEN FROM: "Suicides in India," Maithri, 2011. http://www
.maithrikochi.org/india_suicide_statistics.htm.

This was a period when Monsanto and its Indian partner, Mahyco, were also carrying out illegal field experiments with genetically engineered Bt cotton. All imports and field trials of genetically engineered organisms in India are governed by a provision of the Environment Protection Act called the "Rules for the Manufacture Use, Import, Export, and Storage of Hazardous Microorganisms, Genetically Engineered Organisms, or Cells." We at the Research Foundation for Science, Technology, and Ecology used the law to stop Monsanto's commercialization of Bt cotton in 1999, which is why approval was not granted for commercial sales until 2002.

Rising production costs and falling prices for their products is a recipe for indebtedness, and debt is the main cause of farmers' suicides. This is why the suicides are most prevalent in the cotton belt on which the seed industries' claim is rapidly becoming a stranglehold.

The Failure of Technology

At the start, the technology for engineering Bt genes into cotton was aimed primarily at controlling pests. However, new pests have emerged in Bt cotton, leading to higher use of pesticides. In the Vidarbha region of Maharashtra, which has the highest number of suicides, the area under Bt cotton has increased from 0.2 million hectares in 2004 to 2.88 million hectares in 2007. The cost of pesticides for farmers has increased 13-fold in the same period.

A pest control technology that fails to control pests might be good for seed corporations that are also agrichemical corporations. For farmers, it translates into suicide.

Technologies are tools. When the tool fails, it needs to be replaced. Bt cotton technology has failed to control pests or secure farmers' lives and livelihoods, it is time to replace GM [genetically modified] technology with ecological farming. It is time to stop the killing.

Canada Is Plagued by Aboriginal Youth Suicides

Juhie Bhatia

Juhie Bhatia is a writer and the public health editor of Global Voices. *In the following viewpoint, she investigates the youth suicide crisis in aboriginal communities across Canada, contending that the rates of suicide for First Nations and Inuit young people are much higher than for non-aboriginal youth. Bhatia states that a number of factors contribute to the problem of aboriginal suicides, including isolation, poverty, poor health care, and a lack of mental health outreach and other social services.*

As you read, consider the following questions:

1. How much higher are suicide rates for First Nations youth than non-aboriginal youth, according to Bhatia?

2. According to the viewpoint, how many aboriginal children were required to attend Christian schools from the nineteenth century until the 1970s?

3. What percentage of aboriginal people are under twenty-three years old, according to the author?

When the Vancouver 2010 Winter Olympic Games kick off next month [February 2010], an Aboriginal symbol will be representing the event. The Games' logo is a contem-

Juhie Bhatia, "Canada: Aboriginal Youth Suicides Hit Crisis Rate," *Global Voices in English*, January 18, 2010. www.globalvoicesonline.org. This article by Julia Bhatia was originally published by Global Voices Online, a website that translates and reports on blogs from around the world. Reprinted by permission of Global Voices Online.

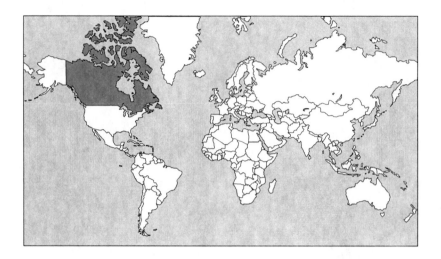

porary inukshuk, a stone sculpture used by Canada's Inuit people as directional landmarks, which organizers say symbolizes friendship and hope. But hope is one thing many Aboriginal youth in Canada appear to lack, as suicide continues to occur at alarming rates, leading to crisis-like situations in some communities.

A Suicide Epidemic in Aboriginal Communities

Suicide rates have declined in Canada through the years but not in Aboriginal communities, though there is great variation among communities. Suicide rates are five to seven times higher for First Nations youth than for non-Aboriginal youth, and rates among Inuit youth are among the highest in the world, at 11 times the national average. Some speculate that the problem is actually worse, as stats don't usually include all Aboriginal groups.

Many factors may be contributing to these high rates, including isolation, poverty and lack of adequate housing, health care, social services and other basic amenities. The blog *Sweetgrass Coaching*, written by Richard Bull, also blames the pain and helplessness that resulted from colonization:

"You can't understand Aboriginal suicide without looking at colonization. We, as indigenous people, must realize that we did not have sky-high suicide rates before the European invasion (contact is too clean a word for what actually happened).

When Canadian society says we're sick that's like a psychopathic killer complaining to someone he's tried to strangle repeatedly that she should do something about the marks on her neck and see a psychiatrist about her recurrent nightmares and low self-esteem."

Specifically, some bloggers point to Canada's residential schools, a federally funded system run by churches that removed Aboriginal children from their families and communities to help them assimilate into Euro-Canadian cultures. From the 19th century until the 1970s, more than 150,000 Aboriginal children were required to attend these Christian schools. It was later revealed that many of these children endured physical, emotional and sexual abuse. In June 2008, Prime Minister Stephen Harper apologized on behalf of the Canadian government and its citizens for the residential school system.

Suicide rates have declined in Canada through the years but not in Aboriginal communities.

The Effects of Residential Schools

Anishinawbe Blog by Bob Goulais says the multigenerational effects of residential schools must not be underestimated.

"Many residential school survivors and their families have no identity beyond their church and what they learned in school. With no identity and without acceptance, they are banished to the margins of society. Although this generation might be more accepting—with access to more social programs and numerous political, legal and rights-based victories—the damage from the past generations has been done. Parents don't know how to be parents. Families don't know how to love. . . .

. . . For far too many youth, suicide is the ultimate way out. We're seeing that more and more in remote, northern communities. This is truly the saddest commentary. I can't imagine how bad life must be for a twelve-year-old Cree boy to hang himself at the recreation centre swing set. To not have the love he needs . . . to not have hope. To know that he hasn't been the first and he won't be the last."

To help combat suicide among Aboriginal youth, the Web site Honouring Life Network, funded by Health Canada, was launched in April 2008. It contains resources for youth and youth workers, a blog and personal stories from Aboriginal youth, among other things. In this personal story a young man talks about how his older brother's death led him to contemplate taking his own life.

"On the second anniversary of his death, I just couldn't feel like missing him anymore. I got up really early in the morning and was walking to the picnic shelter by the lake. This other guy had hung himself there not long before. I felt like I wanted the lake to be the last thing I saw.

My neighbour was out though and started talking to me and I guess he could tell something was wrong. He kept talking to me and talking to me and then he woke up my parents. I never actually told them what I was going to do but they knew somehow. It was a big shock to all of us and it woke us up.

We started to get into the traditional healing; like my dad and I will do a sweat lodge [a ceremonial sauna] with the other men. I'm not going to talk about that because it's private. And my mom does the whole thing with burning sage and sweetgrass, which kind of stinks up the house but that's okay I guess because she's more like my mom again."

Last fall, the Honouring Life Network announced a video contest, where Aboriginal youth were encouraged to submit a short video related to suicide prevention and awareness. The entries can be viewed on their YouTube channel; the winning entry is entitled "Choose Life."

Suicide intervention and prevention can only be successful by taking into account the interconnected relationships between culture, community and environment.

Other Efforts to Help

Other youth are also working to help fight this growing problem. In 2006, Steve Sanderson, an Aboriginal youth cartoonist, wrote and illustrated a comic book called *Darkness Calls* to highlight suicide among Aboriginal youth. Revolving around a teen named Kyle, the story is also available as a video. In the blog *Stageleft*, the blogger discusses 12 other Aboriginal youth who are making a difference, and were rewarded for doing so, including his daughter Charlotte:

> "I feel very safe in saying that not one of the 12 people on the stage lived the lives they have lived, or did the things that they have done, so they could get an award. . . . Charlotte has been concerned with Aboriginal youth suicide rates, the rate of suicide in the Aboriginal community is many times higher than the national rate, and the rate of suicide within the Inuit community is the highest in Canada. To help bring attention to this she, and 4 other Aboriginal youth, walked from Duncan BC [British Columbia] to Ottawa speaking at community centres, youth detention facilities, friendship centres, municipal councils, and to every politician that would listen to them."

A 2009 UNICEF [the United Nations Children's Fund] Canada report on Aboriginal children's health states that suicide intervention and prevention can only be successful by taking into account the interconnected relationships between culture, community and environment. Whatever the approach, the blog *Rebel Youth* says Aboriginal youth, like all Canadian youth, deserve a future.

> "Over 50% of Aboriginal people are under 23. Canadian youth are justified by being deeply enraged by the treatment of Aboriginal peoples by the Canadian ruling class; the attack on Aboriginal youth is an attack on all youth.
>
> Aboriginal youth need a future. A future free from racism, a future with a good paying job, a future with land or proper compensation for land use. A future with rights to universal education right up to and including postsecondary education. A future with good housing. A future without racist police brutality and racial profiling. A future with a dream. A future that is a reality."

Periodical and Internet Sources Bibliography

The following articles have been selected to supplement the diverse views presented in this chapter.

Pia Chandavarkar	"Surge in Suicide Rates Among Indian Youth," *Deutsche Welle*, February 18, 2010. www.dw-world.de.
Dan Haesler	"It's Time to Confront the Deadliest Demon of Them All," *Sydney Morning Herald*, November 3, 2010.
Ofri Ilani	"Of Israel's 400 Yearly Suicides, 75% Are Men," *Haaretz*, July 15, 2009.
Kang Kyung-hee	"Korea Has to End the Suicide Epidemic," *Chosun Ilbo*, April 7, 2010.
Lynne O'Donnell	"Desperation Drives Afghan Women to Suicide by Fire," *Mail & Guardian*, September 30, 2010.
Onora O'Neill	"Real Life Is Too Complex," *Guardian*, July 30, 2010.
Lynn Peeples	"Do Suicide Rates Climb at High Altitudes?" *Reuters*, September 29, 2010. www.reuters.com.
Ayanawo Farada Sanbetu	"Ministry: Suicide Twice as Likely for Ethiopians," *Haaretz*, March 15, 2007.
Allie Tempus	"A Tribal Tragedy: Suicide Rates Soar Among Native Americans," *Wisconsin Center for Investigative Journalism*, November 29, 2010.
Phil Zabriskie	"The Mysteries of the Suicide Tourist," *New York*, May 11, 2008.

CHAPTER 2

Policies to Address Suicide

The European Union Formulates a Plan to Address Its Suicide Problem

Kristian Wahlbeck and Mia Mäkinen

Kristian Wahlbeck and Mia Mäkinen work for the European Commission. In the following viewpoint, they determine that mental health is a human right and that decisive political steps need to be taken to make it a priority among European Union member countries. Wahlbeck and Mäkinen outline five priority action areas: prevention of depression and suicide; mental health in youth and education; mental health in workplace settings; mental health of older people; and combating stigma and social exclusion.

As you read, consider the following questions:

1. According to the authors, how many citizens in the European Union (EU) experience mental disorders?
2. How many suicides are there a year in the EU, according to the viewpoint?
3. What percentage of mental disorders have their onset during adolescence, according to the authors?

Mental health is a human right. It enables citizens to enjoy well-being, quality of life and health. It promotes learning, working and participation in society.

Kristian Wahlbeck and Mia Mäkinen, "Prevention of Depression and Suicide," European Commission, 2008. www.ec.europa.eu. This material is in the public domain.

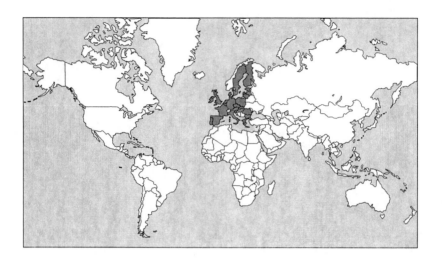

The level of mental health and well-being in the population is a key resource for the success of the EU [European Union] as a knowledge-based society and economy. It is an important factor for the realisation of the objectives . . . on growth and jobs, social cohesion and sustainable development.

Mental disorders are on the rise in the EU. Today, almost 50 million citizens (about 11% of the population) are estimated to experience mental disorders, with women and men developing and exhibiting different symptoms. Depression is already the most prevalent health problem in many EU member states.

The level of mental health and well-being in the population is a key resource for the success of the EU as a knowledge-based society and economy.

Suicide remains a major cause of death. In the EU, there are about 58,000 suicides per year of which 3/4 are committed by men. Eight member states are amongst the fifteen countries with the highest male suicide rates in the world.

Mental disorders and suicide cause immense suffering for individuals, families and communities, and mental disorders are major causes of disability. They put pressure on health, educational, economic, labour market and social welfare systems across the EU.

Complementary action and a combined effort at EU level can help member states tackle these challenges by promoting good mental health and well-being in the population, strengthening preventive action and self-help, and providing support to people who experience mental health problems and their families, further to the measures which member states undertake through health and social services and medical care.

The EU Needs to Take Action

There is a need for a decisive political step to make mental health and well-being a key priority.

Action for mental health and well-being at EU level needs to be developed by involving the relevant policy makers and stakeholders, including those from the health, education, social and justice sectors, social partners, as well as civil society organisations.

People who have experienced mental health problems have valuable expertise and need to play an active role in planning and implementing actions.

Action for mental health and well-being at EU level needs to be developed by involving the relevant policy makers and stakeholders, including those from the health, education, social and justice sectors, social partners, as well as civil society organisations.

The mental health and well-being of citizens and groups, including all age groups, different genders, ethnic origins and socioeconomic groups, needs to be promoted based on targeted interventions that take into account and are sensitive to the diversity of the European population.

There is a need to improve the knowledge base on mental health: by collecting data on the state of mental health in the population and by commissioning research into the epidemiology, causes, determinants and implications of mental health and ill-health, and the possibilities for interventions and best practices in and outside the health and social sectors.

Prevention of Depression and Suicide

Depression is one of the most common and serious mental disorders and a leading risk factor for suicidal behaviour. Every 9 minutes a citizen dies as a consequence of suicide in the EU. The number of suicide attempts is estimated to be ten times higher. Reported rates of suicide in member states differ by a factor 12.

Policy makers and stakeholders are invited to take action on the prevention of suicide and depression including the following:

- Improve the training of health professionals and key actors within the social sector on mental health;

- Restrict access to potential means for suicide;

- Take measures to raise mental health awareness in the general public, among health professionals and other relevant sectors;

- Take measures to reduce risk factors for suicide such as excessive drinking, drug abuse and social exclusion, depression and stress;

- Provide support mechanisms after suicide attempts and for those bereaved by suicide, such as emotional support helplines.

Mental Health in Youth and Education

The foundation of lifelong mental health is laid in the early years. Up to 50% of mental disorders have their onset during

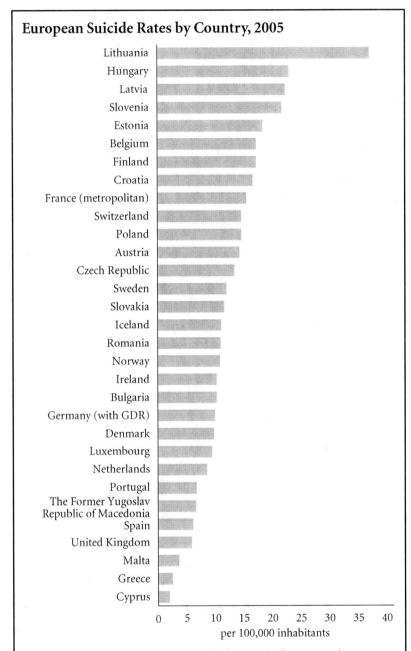

European Suicide Rates by Country, 2005

TAKEN FROM: "Death due to Suicide, by Gender," Eurostat. http://epp .eurostat.ec.europa.eu/tgm/table.do?tab=table&plugin=1&language= en&pcode=tps00122.

adolescence. Mental health problems can be identified in between 10% and 20% of young people, with higher rates among disadvantaged population groups.

Policy makers and stakeholders are invited to take action on mental health in youth and education including the following:

- Ensure schemes for early intervention throughout the educational system;

- Provide programmes to promote parenting skills;

- Promote training of professionals involved in the health, education, youth and other relevant sectors in mental health and well-being;

- Promote the integration of socio-emotional learning into the curricular and extracurricular activities and the cultures of preschools and schools;

- Programmes to prevent abuse, bullying, violence against young people and their exposure to social exclusion;

- Promote the participation of young people in education, culture, sport and employment.

Mental Health in Workplace Settings

Employment is beneficial to physical and mental health. The mental health and well-being of the workforce is a key resource for productivity and innovation in the EU. The pace and nature of work is changing, leading to pressures on mental health and well-being. Action is needed to tackle the steady increase in work absenteeism and incapacity, and to utilize the unused potential for improving productivity that is linked to stress and mental disorders. The workplace plays a central role in the social inclusion of people with mental health problems.

Policy makers, social partners and further stakeholders are invited to take action on mental health at the workplace including the following:

- Improve work organisation, organisational cultures and leadership practices to promote mental well-being at work, including the reconciliation of work and family life;

- Implement mental health and well-being programmes with risk assessment and prevention programmes for situations that can cause adverse effects on the mental health of workers (stress, abusive behaviour such as violence or harassment at work, alcohol, drugs) and early intervention schemes at workplaces;

- Provide measures to support the recruitment, retention or rehabilitation and return to work of people with mental health problems or disorders.

The mental health and well-being of the workforce is a key resource for productivity and innovation in the EU.

Mental Health of Older People

The EU population is ageing. Old age can bring with it certain risk factors for mental health and well-being, such as the loss of social support from families and friends and the emergence of physical or neurodegenerative illness, such as Alzheimer's disease and other forms of dementia. Suicide rates are high in older people. Promoting healthy and active ageing is one of the EU's key policy objectives.

Policy makers and stakeholders are invited to take action on mental health of older people including the following:

- Promote the active participation of older people in community life, including the promotion of their physical activity and educational opportunities;

- Develop flexible retirement schemes which allow older people to remain at work longer on a full-time or part-time basis;

- Provide measures to promote mental health and well-being among older people receiving care (medical and/or social) in both community and institutional settings;

- Take measures to support carers.

Combating Stigma and Social Exclusion

Stigma and social exclusion are both risk factors and consequences of mental disorders, which may create major barriers to help-seeking and recovery.

Policy makers and stakeholders are invited to take action to combat stigma and social exclusion including the following:

- Support anti-stigma campaigns and activities such as in media, schools and at the workplace to promote the integration of people with mental disorders;

- Develop mental health services which are well integrated in the society, put the individual at the centre and operate in a way which avoids stigmatisation and exclusion;

- Promote active inclusion of people with mental health problems in society, including improvement of their access to appropriate employment, training and educational opportunities;

- Involve people with mental health problems and their families and carers in relevant policy and decision-making processes.

The European Pact for Mental Health and Well-Being

The pact recognises that primary responsibility for action in this area rests with member states. However, the pact builds on the EU's potential to inform, promote best practice and encourage actions by member states and stakeholders and help address common challenges and tackle health inequalities.

The reference context for the pact is the EU policy acquis on mental health and well-being that has emerged through initiatives across community policies over the past years, together with the commitments which member states' ministers of health made under the WHO [World Health Organization] Mental Health Declaration for Europe of 2005 and relevant international acts such as the United Nations Convention on the Rights of Persons with Disabilities.

The pact brings together European institutions, member states, stakeholders from relevant sectors, including people at risk of exclusion for mental health reasons, and the research community to support and promote mental health and well-being. It is a reflection of their commitment to a longer-term process of exchange, cooperation and coordination on key challenges.

The pact should facilitate the monitoring of trends and activities in member states and among stakeholders. Based on European best practice, it should help deliver recommendations for action for progress in addressing its priority themes.

African Development and Poverty Programs Must Improve Mental Health Services

Charissa Sparks

Charissa Sparks is a contributor to MediaGlobal, a nonprofit news agency. In the following viewpoint, she reports on a recent report by the World Health Organization that reveals too many Africans suffering from mental health disorders are being underserved by the majority of development and poverty programs. The report determines that governments, nongovernmental organizations, and mental health stakeholders must act to increase funding to provide basic services for Africans who need them.

As you read, consider the following questions:

1. According to the viewpoint, what percentage of the global burden of disease is caused by mental and substance use disorders?

2. What percentage of people with mental disabilities in low- and middle-income countries do not have access to any form of quality treatment, according to Sparks?

3. According to the author, what is the unemployment rate for people with mental disorders?

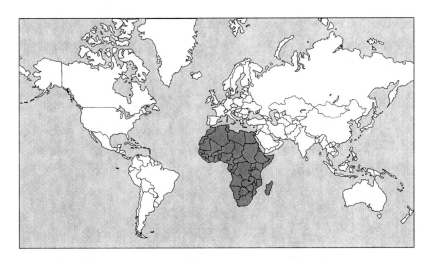

According to a new report released by the World Health Organization (WHO), people suffering with mental health disorders are being overlooked by the majority of development and poverty programs.

Dr. Michelle Funk, coordinator of mental health policy and substance abuse department at WHO, told MediaGlobal, "While mental and substance use disorders account for 13 percent of the global burden of disease, up to 85 percent of people with mental disabilities in low- and middle-income countries do not have access to any form of quality treatment."

Mental illnesses are serious medical conditions that cannot be overcome through "willpower" and are not related to a person's character or intelligence.

Mental disabilities can be extremely debilitating, Funk explained, causing severe distress for the individual, significantly impairing their relationships with others and possibly affecting their concentration, motivation, and self-esteem.

If left untreated, people with mental disorders may have high rates of unemployment, substance abuse, homelessness, and suicide. With global unemployment rates high, it is likely to further set back those with mental disabilities.

"Stigma and discrimination is extremely common, leading to the exclusion and marginalization of persons with mental disabilities," said Funk.

As a result, persons with mental disorders have significantly elevated levels of unemployment, with rates as high as 90 percent. They often have limited access to education and their poorer overall health places them at a much higher risk of poverty. Funk explained, "Persons with mental disabilities who are already in poverty find it much more difficult to improve their quality of life, especially when development programs continue to ignore or exclude this vulnerable group."

Mental illnesses are serious medical conditions that cannot be overcome through "willpower" and are not related to a person's character or intelligence.

Although there are significant consequences for not obtaining treatment, there are a number of reasons why a person may not be able to receive that care.

The main reason is that care is limited. Mental health services are not commonly offered through primary care. This means they must search for outside assistance, which can be expensive, bring attention to their disability, and cause problems for the individual when they reintegrate into their community after treatment.

If they have found a way to obtain the treatment, Funk said, "The quality of mental health services in many countries may be extremely poor."

Dr. Robert Dinerstein, professor of law at the American University and director of the Disability Rights Law Clinic, told MediaGlobal, "History is full of stories, in every country in the world, of individuals who were committed for a short-term hospitalization that later turned into many years of neglectful, abusive institutionalization."

Building and Reinforcing African Health Systems

Many people living in the African region, particularly those in rural areas, often have to travel long distances to receive basic health care. Once they reach a hospital or clinic, they may only receive health care if they pay for it out of their own pockets. Inevitably, many people forego treatment because they cannot afford it, while those who pay may find the costs ruinous and the quality of services limited. Either way, people face impoverishment through incapacitating illness or catastrophic expenditures. Some countries, including Ghana, Kenya, Nigeria and Zambia, are developing national social health insurance schemes to help people cover their health costs.

One long-term solution to these problems, which are common in the African region, lies in further health sector reform, calling for increased financing and more effective use of funds combined with better governance and improved access to affordable interventions that are known to work. A key element of this reform is to establish health districts as the basis for health service delivery. Once established as such, health districts across the region need to be made fully functional so that they can deliver essential health care services to people in an appropriate, affordable and effective manner.

World Health Organization,
The African Regional Health Report:
The Health of the People, *2006.*

Not only are the patients caught in these hospitals for extended periods of time, but "because of lack of resources or lack of imagination, mental health providers too often assume that the only available treatment for a mental disorder is a eupeptic medication (psychiatric drugs)," Dinerstein explained.

"Although these drugs can be helpful in some circumstances and for some patients, they do not cure the underlying mental disorder and often have very serious side effects, to which many patients object."

Even if the patient does object, persons with mental disabilities are frequently denied the legal right to make choices about personal, medical, and financial affairs.

Sylvester Katontoka, president of the Mental Health Users Network of Zambia said, "The time has come when we need to work together to ensure that people with mental health disabilities are given a chance to enjoy life. We must raise our voices and help these people swim out of this life of misery, giving them a taste of a better life."

While skeptics question the cost of treatment, a study conducted by WHO showed that low-income countries can provide help for schizophrenia, bipolar disorder, depression, and hazardous alcohol use for as low as 20 cents per person per year.

"With the right kinds of supports and treatment, many individuals with mental disorders can live productive, fruitful lives. Without such supports, they can find themselves locked away in institutions, needlessly restrained, overmedicated, abused and neglected," Dinerstein said.

The World Health Organization is urging governments, donors, and mental health stakeholders to increase funding and basic mental health services to close this significant treatment gap.

A Chinese Company Acts to Address a Rash of Suicides

Gillian Wong

Gillian Wong is a reporter for Associated Press in Hong Kong. In the following viewpoint, she outlines the policies taken by the Chinese manufacturer Foxconn Technology Group after a series of suicides at its Chinese factories, including raising workers' wages, installing safety nets on buildings to catch jumpers, and holding rallies to raise the morale of workers. Wong reports that labor activists believe the measures do not go far enough and that deeper and more thorough reforms are needed.

As you read, consider the following questions:

1. At the time the viewpoint was written, how many suicides had occurred at Foxconn factories in China?
2. Where have most of the suicides taken place, according to Wong?
3. According to the viewpoint, what do labor activists cite as the reason for the suicide epidemic?

Following a string of suicides at its Chinese factories, Foxconn Technology Group raised workers' wages and installed safety nets on buildings to catch would-be jumpers. Now the often secretive manufacturer of the iPhone and other electronics is holding rallies for its workers to raise morale at the heavily regimented factories.

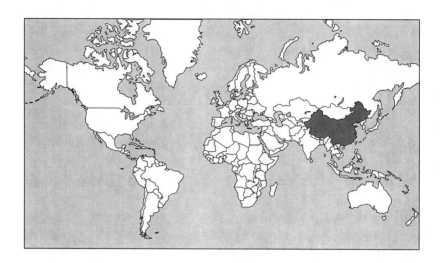

The outreach to workers shows how Foxconn has been shaken by the suicides and the bad press they have attracted to the normally publicity-shy company. The latest suicide—the 12th this year—occurred August 4 when a 22-year-old woman jumped from her factory dormitory in eastern Jiangsu Province.

The motivational rallies are titled "Treasure Your Life, Love Your Family, Care for Each Other to Build a Wonderful Future" and will be held at all facilities in China, according to Burson-Marsteller, a public relations firm representing Foxconn.

The troubles at Foxconn . . . highlighted Chinese workers growing dissatisfaction with the low wages and pressure cooker working conditions that helped turn the country into an international manufacturing powerhouse.

"Foxconn feels it's perhaps time to look back and to learn from the tragedies and to send an important message to their employees that they are not alone, and that the Foxconn family is there to support them and to help them through their challenges," Burson-Marsteller said in an e-mail. The e-mail

The Foxconn Suicides

The deaths have triggered a debate about whether they are an epidemic of mass hysteria—each new suicide copying the death of the last—or a form of social protest. The deaths spotlight the pressure felt by a new generation of employees to work harder and make more money to keep up with China's dizzying pace of growth.

Barbara Demick and David Sarno,
"Firm Shaken by Suicides,"
Los Angeles Times, *May 26, 2010.*

invited reporters to attend a rally later Wednesday at its mammoth industrial park in Shenzhen, which employs 300,000 and where most of the suicides took place.

Foxconn, part of Taiwan's Hon Hai Precision Industry Co., has built itself into the world's largest contract maker of electronics, by delivering quality products on thin profit margins for its customers which include Apple Inc., Sony Corp., Dell Inc., Nokia Corp. and Hewlett-Packard Co.

Labor activists, however, say that success has come in part from driving workers hard by enforcing a rigid management style, operating a too-fast assembly line and requiring excessive overtime. The company denies that it treats employees inhumanely and has pledged to prevent more suicides and improve worker well-being.

The troubles at Foxconn came to light amid high-profile labor unrest in China and highlighted Chinese workers growing dissatisfaction with the low wages and pressure cooker working conditions that helped turn the country into an international manufacturing powerhouse.

One activist said Foxconn's Wednesday rally was unlikely to boost morale and does not replace the need for more thoroughgoing reforms.

"I don't think today's event is going to achieve anything except provide a bit of theater," said Geoffrey Crothall, spokesman of the China Labor Bulletin, a labor rights group based in Hong Kong. "Basically what Foxconn needs to do is treat its workers like decent human beings and pay them a decent wage. It's not rocket science."

"They're still tackling this from a top-down approach, they are organizing the workers. They're not allowing the workers to organize themselves," Crothall said.

A similar gathering was held Monday at Foxconn's campus in the northern city of Taiyuan, which employs about 60,000 workers. A Foxconn official in Taipei said the company decided that day to remove safety nets from the Taiyuan plant, although there are no plans to do the same at its other factories.

In May, Hon Hai's founder Terry Gou promised to work harder to prevent more deaths. More counselors were being hired and employees also were being assigned to 50-person groups to watch one another for signs of emotional trouble.

Foxconn also announced two raises, more than doubling the basic worker pay to 2,000 yuan ($293) a month at the Shenzhen compound. But workers have to pass a three-month review period before they qualify for the second raise.

Canada Considers a Mental Health Plan to Reduce Its Suicide Rate

Charlie Fidelman

Charlie Fidelman is a reporter for the Montreal Gazette. *In the following viewpoint, he details the attempts of suicide prevention groups and mental health advocates to convince Quebec officials to formulate more effective suicide prevention policies instead of focusing on legalizing assisted suicide. Fidelman underscores the belief of many mental health advocates that more resources for those suffering from mental illnesses would effectively and significantly lower the suicide rate in Quebec.*

As you read, consider the following questions:

1. According to Fidelman, how many people die by suicide in Canada every year?
2. How many people in Quebec committed suicide in 2008, according to the viewpoint?
3. How many people in five suffer from a mental disorder, according to the author?

When Nicolas killed himself a day short of his 17th birthday, his mother, Ann Toth, was left to grieve the unbearable loss.

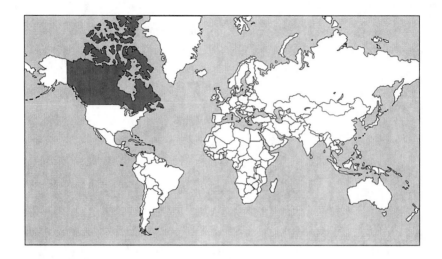

Two years later—as provincial government consultations on assisted suicide finish in Montreal today, coinciding with World Suicide Prevention Day—Toth says the Quebec government should focus resources on training doctors about mental health rather than endorse the use of medicine to help people end their lives.

Toth is not alone. Suicide prevention groups and mental health advocates are calling for better prevention strategies before any steps are taken toward legalizing suicide.

> *Suicide prevention groups and mental health advocates are calling for better prevention strategies before any steps are taken toward legalizing suicide.*

Prioritize Issues

A public discussion about assisted suicide is important, said Marion Cooper, president of the Canadian Association for Suicide Prevention.

"But it's premature to have a position on assisted suicide when we don't have a national strategy on suicide prevention, which is a public health issue," she said.

"It's very dangerous to tread on those topics without an overarching support for suicide prevention. There's a risk that if legislation on assisted suicide were to move forward that it could be misinterpreted and abused."

Suicide in Canada

About 4,000 people die by suicide in Canada every year.

Provincial statistics show a drop of 32 per cent from 1,620 deaths in 1999 to 1,103 in 2008; for men that's down from 1,284 deaths to 842 and in women, 336 deaths to 260.

The real tragedy is that most of these deaths are preventable, Toth said.

"My son didn't see any recourse," she said, adding that the family is still in shock.

"My son wanted to live. The illness that came over him was very quick—five months before he died—and the medical profession failed him."

It's not clear if he suffered from schizophrenia.

After three weeks at the Douglas Hospital, Nicolas came out with a diagnosis of "a psychosis of some kind," Toth said, anti-psychotic medication but no follow-up.

Two months after the crisis, he took bullets found on a farm, reassembled a hunting gun at his father's house and shot himself.

More Resources Needed

Toth says she understands those who support euthanasia because they want to control the time and circumstances of their own death.

But maybe if there were more resources available for patients and families with mental illnesses, she said, her son would still be alive today.

"Our doctors don't have time to give support" or even information about where to find support, she said.

Ten Tips for Mental Health

1. Build Confidence
Identify your abilities and weaknesses ... and do the best with what you have.

2. Eat Right, Keep Fit
A balanced diet, exercise and rest can help you to reduce stress and enjoy life.

3. Make Time for Family and Friends
These relationships need to be nurtured. . . .

4. Give and Accept Support
Friends and family relationships thrive when they are "put to the test."

5. Create a Meaningful Budget
Financial problems cause stress. Overspending ... is often the culprit.

6. Volunteer
Being involved in community gives a sense of purpose. . . .

7. Manage Stress
We all have stressors ... learning how to deal with them ... will maintain our mental health.

8. Find Strength in Numbers
Sharing a problem with others ... will make you feel less isolated.

9. Identify and Deal with Moods
We all need to find safe and constructive ways to express our feelings of anger, sadness, joy and fear.

10. Learn to Be at Peace with Yourself
Get to know who you are ... and learn to balance what you can and cannot change about yourself.

Canadian Mental Health Association, "10 Tips for Mental Health," 2010. Copyright © 2010 by Canadian Mental Health Association. All rights reserved. Reprinted by permission.

"Nobody, not a doctor, not a nurse, not a psychiatrist, a psychologist, the janitor or the concierge gave me anywhere to go," she recalled.

Suicide Prevention Should Be Improved

The hearings by a panel of Quebec legislators on end-of-life issues are a good thing, said Bruno Marchand of the Association québécoise de prévention du suicide.

"But if we put as much money into prevention, we'd really have an impact on suicide prevention," he said.

One in five people suffers from a mental disorder.

People who are asking for assisted suicide because of chronic illnesses, paralysis or pain are making a clear choice, Toth said: "I don't feel my son made a conscious choice. The old Nicolas we knew and loved would never have made that decision. He had too much to live for."

South Africa Should Craft a National Mental Health Strategy to Decrease Teen Suicides

Valencia Talane

Valencia Talane is a columnist for Mail & Guardian. *In the following viewpoint, she expresses her surprise and concern over learning that a young family member had tried to commit suicide twice in the past two years. Talane reports that many parents dealing with suicidal teenagers don't recognize the warning signs and argues that there should be more resources in South Africa to help teens and parents.*

As you read, consider the following questions:

1. According to Talane, what percentage of all teenage deaths in South Africa are suicides?
2. What percentage of overall deaths in South Africa are suicides, according to the author?
3. According to the viewpoint, what do studies show about the warning signs among depressed teenagers?

A 15-year-old family member of mine has allegedly attempted, not once, but twice, to end her life in the last two years.

Valencia Talane, "Tackling Teenage Suicide in South Africa," *The Mail & Guardian Online*, November 18, 2009. www.mg.co.za. Copyright © 2009 by *The Mail & Guardian Online*. All rights reserved. Reprinted by permission.

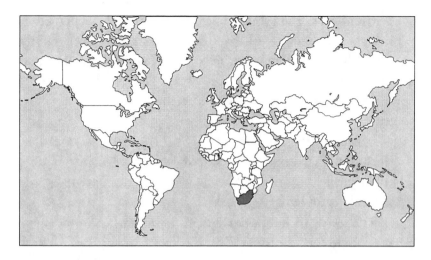

I found this out recently. The notes she had written highlighting the issues in her life were found by her mother, my cousin, on both occasions.

Just as with many other issues, I had not given the issue of teenage suicide in South Africa a lot of thought until it hit close to home.

Maybe it's because we're nearing the matric-result [graduation exam] time of the year, or maybe I'm just flushed over hearing of such news within my own family, but I have been thinking a lot about what causes young people to take their own lives, as well as what is being done—or not done—about it.

> *I had not given the issue of teenage suicide in South Africa a lot of thought until it hit close to home.*

Confronting the Problem

I have no idea what I would do if, in the midst of raising a teenage girl, I discovered that she was not only unhappy with her life, but that she was so unhappy that she was willing to see it come to an end.

I would have thought a mother who finds herself in that position would require all the strength and support of family and friends, not to mention help in the form of professional advice. To my greatest surprise, my cousin decided that despite the magnitude of this crisis, it made sense to keep it a secret.

Her decision has gnawed at me for a few days. More than the fact that there may be a suicidal teenager in my family, what concerns me is the lack of action from her parents at addressing the problem.

There seems to be a preoccupation with what would happen if people found out.

That their daughter is having to resort to getting their attention in the most disturbing way is in itself a warning, to say the least, and I personally find it almost criminal that they are not rolling up their sleeves, getting their hands dirty and getting to the bottom of it.

This attitude of keeping it within the family got me thinking of how many other parents approach crisis situations of this kind in the same way. Statistics shout at us from every direction, cautioning us to be aware of the signs of a depressed and suicidal teenager, but these go unnoticed or ignored.

Suicide Trends in South Africa

Nine percent of all teenage deaths reported in the country annually are suicides. This is according to the South African Depression and Anxiety Group (Sadag). It also says these suicides make up 6% of the overall number annually. Furthermore, numerous studies have revealed that signs among depressed teenagers are usually distinct and visible enough for parents and other adults within the family to detect.

Still, the numbers rise, the pressure mounts and the only active effort in South Africa that is aimed specifically at tackling the issue of teenage suicides is Sadag's Suicide Shouldn't Be a Secret programme.

South African Cities and Methods of Suicide

	Johannesburg	eThekwini	Cape Town	Tshwane	Nelson Mandela	Buffalo City	Total Cities
Hanging (%)	38.2	54.4	44.1	28.9	47.1	55.1	43.2
Firearm (%)	32.0	23.5	25.7	42.1	19.5	21.5	28.9
Poison (%)	11.1	10.2	15.9	12.5	21.4	8.6	12.6
Other (%)	18.7	11.9	14.4	16.5	12.0	14.9	15.3
Number of Deaths	**1,455**	**1,136**	**869**	**799**	**384**	**303**	**4,946**

TAKEN FROM: Stephanie Burrows and Lucie Laflamme, "Suicide Mortality in South Africa," *Social Psychiatry and Psychiatric Epidemiology*, 2006.

From my cousin's reaction to her daughter's crisis, and her subsequent behaviour, I gather that many parents out there are either unaware or ignorant of the alarm bells of the depressed teenager.

The issue stems from families not communicating important matters affecting their members, young and old, and taking for granted what problems, if any, the younger members of the family are able to not only detect, but to take on as added pressure in their own lives.

Some parents could be ignorant of the effects of the family's financial stresses on their teenagers, who may in turn feel somewhat responsible for the situation. Another common scenario is when the younger family members find it hard to deal with the death or illness of a parent or sibling, and find that they cannot talk to the adults in their lives about it and therefore have to find their own way of grieving.

However, there is also a need to look at the situation from a broader point of view, that of the nation, to come up with a national solution to a national problem.

If the numbers mentioned above are anything to go by, we as a country are failing our teenagers in a big way.

Could we possibly start in the home and work our way out?

Britain Should Legalize Assisted Suicide

Joel Joffe

Joel Joffe is a human rights lawyer. In the following viewpoint, he urges the legalization of assisted suicide in Britain, arguing that it would be a compassionate and ethical policy that would allow mentally competent individuals to control their own lives. Joffe stresses that there would have to be strong protections in place for vulnerable citizens to ensure that they are not pressured to end their lives before they are ready.

As you read, consider the following questions:

1. According to Joffe, what is the punishment in Britain for assisted suicide?
2. Why does the author believe that those involved in the medical professions should not be responsible for granting approval for the assistance to die?
3. Who does the author propose make the decision for approval in assisted suicide situations?

For the overwhelming majority of terminally ill patients, the solution to their suffering is quality palliative care, which I enthusiastically support. But there is a small but significant minority of terminally ill patients for whom palliative

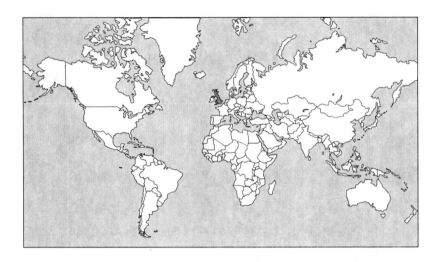

care is not the solution, and who suffer terribly until they die. Some of these people wish to end their suffering by ending their lives, and would like assistance to do this, in a way which would enable them to bring their lives to an end with dignity at a time and place of their choice, which would normally be at home surrounded by their loved ones.

However under our current law, helping even a terminally ill person who is suffering unbearably to die at his or her request, would be a crime punishable under the 1961 Suicide Act with up to 14 years imprisonment.

A Compassionate and Ethical Policy

The only way to prevent such suffering appears to me to be to change the law, so as to allow such patients to lawfully receive assistance to die. Assisted suicide would, in these circumstances, be a compassionate and ethical response to a desperate need. A good rather than a harm, and complementary rather than in opposition to palliative care.

The principle underpinning this proposal to change the law is the human right of all individuals to decide for themselves how to lead their lives, which would include their choice on how and when to die at a time their lives are coming to an end. However, it is clear that this right must be subject to the limitation, that in ending their own lives, patients must not indirectly harm other vulnerable members of society.

It follows that in meeting the need to alleviate the suffering of some individuals, care must be taken not to generally undermine the existing law, which, while allowing suicide, does not aim to encourage it, and protects citizens from being encouraged or influenced to end their lives.

The principle underpinning this proposal to change the law is the human right of all individuals to decide for themselves how to lead their lives, which would include their choice on how and when to die at a time their lives are coming to an end.

A Policy Britain Wants

Proper respect must also be paid to the views of those who are opposed to assisted suicide. However, as a small minority, they should not be allowed, without good reason, to impose their beliefs and views on the majority of society who do not share them.

In the legislation which has previously been proposed, those deciding whether the request for assistance to die gets approval have been members of the medical profession.

However, it has become clear that doctors, nurses and other health practitioners would have grave misgivings about their personal involvement in assisted suicide, often irrespective of whether or not they are opposed to a change in the law. Their instinctive reaction is not to help anyone to end their life, which is understandable as they joined their profession in order to cure or prevent patients from falling ill, and in the cases of terminally ill patients, to ease their suffering in the dying process.

Accordingly, what I now propose is to take doctors out of the investigative and decision-making process, which should become the role of a legal body such as the high court or the court of protection or tribunals specifically set up for this purpose. This would be consistent with the present role of the courts, which decide upon whether patients who have been in a vegetative state for long periods should be allowed to die, and also consistent with the role of the court of protection in determining mental competence in relation to advance directives.

The courts or another legal body would have the responsibility for investigating and determining whether a terminally ill patient suffering unbearably should be entitled to ask for assistance to die. They would be required to make this decision within a framework, which will cover the principles, restrictions and safeguards I have set out.

When authorising assistance to the patient to die, the courts would also authorise the prescription of life-ending medication to the patient, or in the very small number of cases where the patient is so physically disabled that he or she cannot ingest the medication, would authorise such other means of self-administration of the medication as would enable the patient to end his or her life. The key point would be that responsibility for the ultimate act still rested with the patient.

Putting Safeguards in Place

The medication and means would only be made available after a minimum waiting period, and it would be for the patients to decide when to ingest the medication, or to change their minds and not to ingest it at all.

Self-administration is an important safeguard against possible undue influence, as there could be no better evidence of a decision freely and voluntarily made by the patient.

I am not in favour of voluntary euthanasia which is where a third party ends the life of the patient. Because assisted suicide provides a solution to all terminally ill patients who desperately wish to end their suffering, there is nothing to be gained by extending the law to allow voluntary euthanasia as well.

Britain Should Resist Calls to Legalize Assisted Suicide

Cristina Odone

Cristina Odone is an author and broadcaster. In the following viewpoint, she contends that legalizing assisted suicide in Britain would condemn the more vulnerable—the poor, the disabled, and the less articulate—to a premature death. Odone considers legalized assisted suicide as a threat to public safety and argues that the British government should resist calls for the legalization of assisted suicide.

As you read, consider the following questions:

1. According to the author, how much does assisted suicide cost at the Dignitas clinic in Switzerland?
2. What percentage of the British population will be over the age of sixty-five by 2033, according to the viewpoint?
3. What percentage of people in Britain are in favor of the "right to die," according to Odone?

A painless and speedy death, resulting from a hygienic medical procedure that leaves no mess: Assisted suicide is the final consumer fantasy. Although illegal in Britain, it is already available to the determined and comfortably-off, who

Cristina Odone, "Assisted Suicide: How the Chattering Classes Have It Wrong," Centre for Policy Studies, October 2010. www.cps.org.uk. Copyright © 2010 by Centre for Policy Studies. All rights reserved. Reprinted by permission.

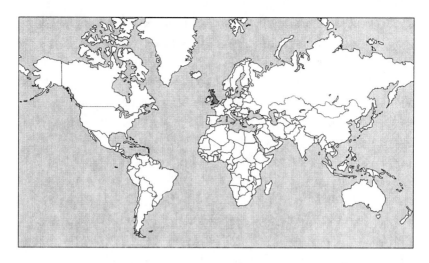

can buy (at £10,000 a shot) an appointment with death at the Dignitas clinic in Switzerland. Here, completely legally, a physician will inject them with a fatal poison. Why can't, argue the distinguished and articulate advocates of assisted suicide and voluntary euthanasia, this choice be available to all?

Protecting the Sick and Disadvantaged

The simple answer is that, if we legalise assisted suicide, we risk having a strident élite condemning the less fortunate to a premature death. For it is the marginalised, the disabled, the less articulate and the poor who are most likely to be under pressure to accelerate their death. The NHS [National Health Service] hospital or care home, engulfed by a rising tide of elderly people, and starved of funds, will feel the burden of the 'bed-blocker'—and fill the insecure and vulnerable patient with guilt for taxing a system that is already under severe strain. Above all, the disadvantaged, fearful of authorities and lost in bureaucracy, may not know how to manipulate the system and may, in comparison to the confident members of the choice-obsessed consumerist élite, be more subject to manipulation by others.

A well-organised lobby of euthanasia supporters, led by Dignity in Dying, have tried to convince us that legalising assisted suicide is the most humane solution for everyone's final exit. Their campaign draws its force not only from the worried well, but also from new, and alarming, demographic forecasts: By 2033, 23% of the population will be over the age of 65. Research undertaken by Barbara Gomes and Professor Irene Higginson suggests that the annual number of deaths is expected to rise by 17% between 2012 and 2030.

This huge new pressure on our health and support systems risks turning our last stage of life, and our death, into a nightmare. There are two dangers: The first is that the needs of those too old and weak to look after themselves may be ignored; the other is that when everyone is competing for limited resources, the aged may feel guilty because they are diverting investments from everyone else.

The simple answer is that, if we legalise assisted suicide, we risk having a strident élite condemning the less fortunate to a premature death.

Demand for Assisted Suicide Rises

The legalisation of assisted suicide and voluntary euthanasia was once thought unthinkable in this country, where it was associated with the Nazis' secret euthanasia programme. Yet public demand for what is being euphemistically called the 'right to die' has grown hugely (to 74%, according to a poll last year by the *Times*). Cases such as Lynne Gilderdale's, who had suffered with a paralyzing form of ME [myalgic encephalopathy], for 17 years, until her mother, Bridget Kathleen Gilderdale, helped her to die by giving her an overdose, have triggered sympathetic reactions; their prosecution has met with huge opposition.

The issue has been debated in Parliament four times over the past six years. Debbie Purdy, who has MS [multiple sclerosis], last year won the right to have the prosecution guidelines affecting those who assist suicide clarified. Keir Starmer QC, the director of public prosecutions (DPP), published his guidelines in February 2010.

Concerns About the Vulnerable

The new guidelines have not paved the way for assisted suicide; they call for each case to be judged on its own merits. But those working with the elderly, the disabled, and the terminally ill worry that, once introduced on compassionate grounds, assisted suicide will lead to death on request or euthanasia without consent.

In particular, they contend that any change in the law will expose the vulnerable to coercion by their family or other interested parties, such as a doctor, or a nursing home director. They are concerned that too many could be talked or pressured into giving up their lives for the convenience of younger, healthier individuals.

Legalising assisted suicide risks harming the most vulnerable. It should be rejected on grounds of public safety, not personal morality.

An Élite Policy

For the real battle over assisted suicide and euthanasia is between the haves and have-nots. Euthanasia enthusiasts such as Lord [Joel] Joffe and Lord [Charles] Falconer (both of whom have attempted in Parliament to legalise assisted suicide) and Dignity in Dying patrons such as Terry Pratchett, AN Wilson and Patricia Hewitt need not fear coercion if assisted suicide becomes legal: articulate, determined and well-connected, they would know how to protect themselves in any situation. But for millions of others, too anxious, inarticulate, or fragile to clearly defend their needs, their disadvantage may cost them their lives. As Dr Carol J Gill has written:

"Viewing the world from a position of privilege may limit one's insight into the consequences of a policy change whose greatest impact could fall on socially marginalised groups."

Not a Religious Issue

The debate about assisted suicide and euthanasia has been portrayed as a battle between religious and anti-religious groups. It is not. Many secularists view assisted suicide and euthanasia with horror; while there are believers who regard assisting someone to end their lives to be an act of charity. Out of the 93 speeches dedicated to this issue in *Hansard* [the printed daily debates in the House of Commons] only 6 are by bishops; the rest are by parliamentarians concerned that a change in the law carries with it the potential for coercion.

If this is to be resolved, it should be on the basis of facts, not faith. Legalising assisted suicide risks harming the most vulnerable. It should be rejected on grounds of public safety, not personal morality.

The Dangers in Legalizing Assisted Suicide

The dangers inherent in the legalisation of assisted suicide can be grouped in four categories:

Second-class human beings

The danger is that less-than-perfect citizens will be deemed expendable. Not only will those who require a great deal of care and assistance, including the elderly, feel that in the new hierarchy promoted by euthanasia they stand at the bottom rung; they may feel guilty, seeing themselves reduced to a burden on their families or the state. This will be all the truer of the socially marginalised.

Doctor death

When the doctor prescribes a fatal potion or administers a lethal injection, rather than battling to save you from disease and/or death, trust in doctor-patient relationships risks being

Euthanasia and Assisted Suicide

Euthanasia which is the active and intentional termination of a person's life remains illegal in the UK [United Kingdom]. It is morally and legally different to the withholding or withdrawal of treatment. Arguments for legalisation of euthanasia are generally based on arguments about competent individuals' rights to choose the manner of their demise or about cases where medicine is unable to control distressing terminal symptoms. Although the BMA [British Medical Association] respects the concept of individual autonomy, it argues that there are limits to what patients can choose if their choice will impact on other people.

Arguments against legalisation often focus on practical points. If euthanasia were an option, there might be pressure for all seriously ill people to consider it even if they would not otherwise entertain such an idea. Health professionals explaining options for the management of terminal illness would have to include an explanation of assisted dying. Patients might feel obliged to choose it for the wrong reasons, if they were worried about being a burden, or concerned about the financial implications of a long terminal illness. Legalisation could generate anxiety for vulnerable, elderly, disabled or very ill patients.

British Medical Association
"End-of-Life Decisions," August 2009.

destroyed. It is precisely because we trust our doctors always to act in our best interests that what is being euphemistically called 'assisted dying' is so dangerous: A doctor who agreed to a patient's request to 'end it all' could all too easily send a signal, however unintended, that the doctor considered death was the best course of action in the patient's circumstances.

The death squad

Who will regulate these deaths, if we don't adopt the physician-assisted suicide model? Assuming we allow for conscientious objectors, a self-selecting cadre of 'death regulators' will take charge of assisted suicide. Who will be able to check this all-powerful death squad? Who can be sure that at the last minute the patient does not undergo a change of heart yet is pushed to go ahead with suicide anyway by those present? None of the scenarios put forward by the euthanasia lobby offer any insurance that coercion will not take place once official approval for an assisted suicide has been given.

Slippery slope

Once assisted suicide becomes legal, it will slide into voluntary euthanasia which in turn will lead to involuntary euthanasia. Physician-assisted suicide is, after all, simply physician-administered euthanasia. Once the principle is breached that a doctor may act knowingly to bring about a patient's death, the way to full-scale euthanasia lies open.

In short, legalising euthanasia will change our lives, forever. Our world will become a harder, more selfish place, where the weak will have no voice and no value. The Government must therefore resist calls for the legalisation of assisted suicide and voluntary euthanasia.

Periodical and Internet Sources Bibliography

The following articles have been selected to supplement the diverse views presented in this chapter.

Anushka Asthana — "Assisted Suicide Law to Be Reviewed by Lords," *Observer*, November 28, 2010.

Kate Benson — "Suicide-Prevention Groups Say Need Is Desperate," *Sydney Morning Herald*, June 28, 2010.

Julie Beun — "Mental Health Requires More Ideas and More Funding," *Montreal Gazette*, February 9, 2011.

Andrew Chambers — "Japan: Ending the Culture of the 'Honourable' Suicide," *Guardian*, August 3, 2010.

James Dao — "Taking Calls from Veterans on the Brink," *New York Times*, July 30, 2010.

Aaron Derfel — "Palliative Care, Not Euthanasia, Needed: Groups," *Montreal Gazette*, February 4, 2011.

Nicole Goebel — "German Court Rules in Favor of Passive Assisted Suicide," Deutsche Welle, June 25, 2010. www.dw-world.de.

Tarryn Harbour — "Recession Depression: Change the Way You Think," *Mail & Guardian*, December 23, 2010.

Adele Horin — "Suicide Can Be Stopped: Lifeline's Message," *Sydney Morning Herald*, January 5, 2010.

Kenneth Maxwell — "Suicide: The $32 Billion Bill Japan Can't Afford," *Wall Street Journal*, September 7, 2010.

National Post — "We Can't Keep Losing Our Youth to Suicide," December 4, 2010.

GLOBALVIEWPOINTS

CHAPTER 3

Political, Social, and Economic Factors Contributing to Suicide

Afghan Women Are Killing Themselves at a High Rate

Sudabah Afzali

Sudabah Afzali is a reporter for the Institute for War & Peace Reporting. In the following viewpoint, Afzali reveals that suicides by women in Herat province in Afghanistan are on the rise. Afzali finds that experts believe the country's repressive, male-dominated society and an absence of options for women often lead many desperate women to turn to suicide.

As you read, consider the following questions:

1. As the author reports, how much has suicide among women in Herat increased from 2009 to 2010?
2. According to Dr. Sayed Naim Alemi, how many cases of attempted suicide through burning and poison had been recorded at his hospital in the past six months?
3. How many of those women died, according to Afzali?

Mahjabin, 23, weeps as she describes the events that led her to attempt suicide by swallowing rat poison. Speaking slowly and with difficulty from her bed in Herat hospital, she said that five years ago, after she returned from living in Iran, her father and brothers prevented her from studying and then forced her into marriage.

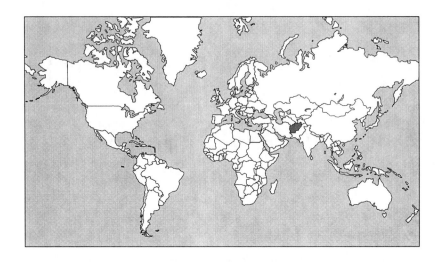

"My family sold me to that man, and married me off to him for money," she sobbed.

Her new husband already had a wife, but as she had not borne him a child, he decided to take another one—a common practice in Afghanistan.

After a year, when Mahjabin had not become pregnant, the abuse began.

In most cases, the women try to kill themselves by pouring fuel over their bodies and setting themselves on fire, although more women are now turning to swallowing chemicals like rat poison.

"My mother-in-law would fight with me every day," she said. "She would ask me sarcastically why I hadn't had a baby. She would say she was going to find another woman for her son. My husband also treated me with anger."

Mahjabin decided to end it all because she had nowhere to turn.

"My family wouldn't support me. I thought that if I went to the authorities, no one would listen to me. I was disappointed on all sides. So I decided to end my life of suffering by taking rat poison."

Mahjabin says she is sorry she was found and taken to hospital in time for her life to be saved.

"If they force me to return to my husband's house," she warned, "I will try to kill myself again."

A Common Solution in Herat

Mahjabin's is not an isolated case. Officials in Herat province say cases of suicide amongst women—already higher in Herat than in other provinces—have increased by 50 per cent over the last year.

In most cases, the women try to kill themselves by pouring fuel over their bodies and setting themselves on fire, although more women are now turning to swallowing chemicals like rat poison.

Dr Sayed Naim Alemi, the director of the regional hospital in Herat, told IWPR [Institute for War & Peace Reporting] that 85 cases of attempted suicide through burning and poison had been recorded at his hospital in the past six months. Out of these, 57 women died.

A Culture Shock

Most of these incidents, he said, involved women recently returned from living in Iran.

"There may [be] the provision needed for women to defend their rights there [in Iran]," he said. "But in Afghanistan, particularly around Herat, women are considered chattels to be sold."

Observers say that in Afghanistan's traditional, male-dominated society, violence against women, combined with the absence of rule of law, means those who face such pressures have no way out and often turn to suicide.

Mohammad Dawud Monir, an expert on social and legal affairs in Herat, noted that returnees from Iran found themselves in a particularly difficult situation.

Why Afghan Women Kill Themselves

There has been little improvement in the lot of women in rural areas despite the introduction of constitutional rights after the Taliban's brutal regime was overthrown in late 2001.

Afghanistan remains a society mired in misogyny, with most women confined to their homes, unsocialised and uneducated, with no control over their lives.

Lynne O'Donnell,
"Desperation Drives Afghan Women to Suicide by Fire,"
Mail & Guardian, *September 30, 2010.*

"Large numbers of people in Herat were forced to leave the country and go to Iran because of the bad situation over the past 30 years, and comparatively, they had a better life there," he explained. "To some extent, they were exposed to technology and civilisation. The women saw the prosperity and rights enjoyed by Iranian women. When they returned, they faced unemployment, poverty and traditional societal restrictions."

Observers say that in Afghanistan's traditional, male-dominated society, violence against women, combined with the absence of rule of law, means those who face such pressures have no way out and often turn to suicide.

Suicide Rate Will Only Get Worse

Hamida Husseini, director of the cultural department of the government directorate for women's affairs in Herat, says that if nothing is done to address the rising number of suicides in the province, the loss of life will reach unacceptable levels.

Her department, she said, along with other government agencies and a number of women's groups, plans to boost public awareness of the problem and lobby for punishment for those who commit violence against women.

They intend to send teams from house to house talking to young mothers and girls about their lives and daily problems. That way, said Husseini, her department will gain a more accurate picture of the situation and will thus be better able to support vulnerable families.

"Older women will be hired for this programme," she said, "because they have some experience and can create good relationships with women and girls, ask about their problems and keep in touch in the long term."

Cultural Aspects of Suicide in Afghanistan

Soraya Pakzad, head of the charity Neda-i Zan [Women's Voice], said violence against women and female suicide are not unique to Herat. The difference, she said was that families elsewhere find it easier to conceal such cases and the media are less likely to report on them.

"Research conducted by legal organisations shows that Kandahar was also among the provinces with a high incidence of female suicide in 2008. But because of the social structure in that province, and because the media's hands were tied, these cases were not publicised very much."

Pakzad argues that because relatively speaking, Herat society is more open, women there are more aware of their rights. But when these rights are denied them, they feel suicide is the only option available to them.

She said Afghanistan's laws setting out women's rights exist only on paper and are generally not put into practice.

Others believe female suicide is rooted in discriminatory customs, poverty and inequality.

Monir said one contributory factor is the practice of marrying girls off to much older husbands against their will, in exchange for money.

Those who go down the arduous path of divorcing their husbands are looked down on and have a hard time in Afghan society. With many doors closed to them, they too may opt for suicide as the only solution.

"The lack of the rule of law paved the way for such shocking cases to happen," said Monir, calling for the Afghan government and the international community to coordinate efforts to identify and address the problems facing women.

Police Deny the Problem Exists

A local police official denied that the authorities ignored violence against women.

Police spokesman Colonel Abdol Rauf Ahmadi said, "Even in cases where the victim in a case of attempted suicide does not make a complaint, the police conduct extensive investigations and arrest any individuals directly or indirectly involved, and hand them over to the judicial authorities."

Many of the survivors, like Mahjabin, regret that their suicide attempts failed.

Among them is Shokria, 28, who suffered 80 per cent burns. Doctors say they will not be able to save her life.

Wrapped in bandages with only her eyes visible, and her speech slurred, Shokria said she was married against her will to a husband who beat her and their children every day.

Her father ignored her appeals, and she says she was unable to get help from women's rights groups, so she decided on suicide.

"I don't regret setting myself on fire," she said. "My only concern is that my children will still be with that cruel man."

Tajikistan's Economic Crisis Leads to Higher Suicide Rate

Bakhtior Valiev

In the following viewpoint, Bakhtior Valiev investigates a series of suicides in northern Tajikistan that have been attributed to economic hardships caused by the global economic downturn. Valiev argues that the suicide rate is worse among men, who bear the responsibility for providing for their families and have few mental health resources for stress and depression. Valiev is a reporter for the Institute for War & Peace Reporting.

As you read, consider the following questions:

1. According to Valiev, how many seasonal workers from Soghd are working abroad?
2. From January–June 2009, how many suicides in Soghd were caused directly by the economic crisis, as the author reports?
3. According to the author, how many suicides were there overall in Soghd during that period?

Economic hardship resulting from the global financial crisis is to blame for a spate of suicides in the northern Tajikistan region of Soghd, victims' relatives and experts say.

A mother of three who lives in the provincial capital Khujand said her car-dealer husband committed suicide after some of his clients failed to pay him.

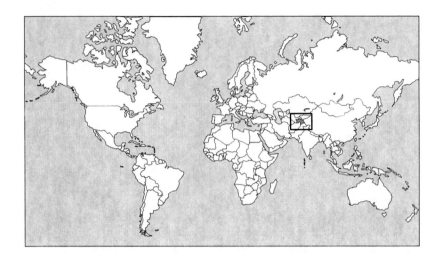

"He was in the business of buying and selling imported cars. He took loans, a lot of money. He did not tell me about his problems but I understood that he had been simply let down," she said.

On top of her bereavement, the woman has had to deal with some of her husband's creditors. "Now they come to me and demand that I repay his debts.

"Where do I get this kind of money? If I had been working I would have tried to pay it back little by little. It is good that others have cancelled his debts."

Another Tragic Case

A mother of two from Bobojon Gafurov district not far from Khujand lost her husband of 11 years.

They shared a house with his two brothers and their families. While her husband was working they managed to make ends meet but things changed when he lost his job.

"His brothers did not like it and told us to move out. My husband did not see any way out and hanged himself," she said.

"After the 40-day mourning period, they [the brothers] threw me out of the house. It was a terrible time for me. I went to live with my relatives, and then with my sister. Kind people gave me a helping hand and found me a place in a hostel. I found a job to feed my children."

Suicides Attributed to Economic Factors

The Soghd region, traditionally better off than other parts of the country thanks to its industry, has been hit hard by the economic downturn.

The crisis has not only cut local incomes and the number of jobs but also remittances from thousands of labour migrants. Some 150,000 seasonal workers from Soghd are working abroad, mostly in Russia but also in Kazakhstan, according to official figures.

Najiba Shirinbekova, who heads a nongovernmental group called Law and Prosperity, told IWPR [Institute for War & Peace Reporting], "The latest information indicates a particularly high level of poverty in the region. This is because factories are standing idle because of the financial crisis and the winter energy crisis."

In the first six months of the year, labour migrants from Soghd sent home more than 200 million US dollars, compared with last year, when the figure for the same period was more than 300 million dollars.

Assessing the Scope of the Problem

There are no official records of how many suicide cases are directly caused by the economic crisis, though police sometimes note "financial problems" when recording deaths.

From January till the end of June [2009], the number is given as 15. However, the figures do not distinguish between those living in long-term poverty and those whose dire financial situation has been compounded by the economic slowdown.

The interior ministry office in Soghd said that in the first six months of the year police registered 92 cases of suicide and 52 attempted suicides, 25 more than the figures for the same period last year.

Despite a lack of clarity in suicide statistics, there are some indications that people are taking their lives under the stress caused by the economic crisis.

There are no official records of how many suicide cases are directly caused by the economic crisis, though police sometimes note "financial problems" when recording deaths.

The Gender Difference

There are more men than women who committed or attempted suicide—84 and 78 respectively. Many men are of working age and the country has more women than men because of the numbers working abroad.

An expert in gender issues, Rano Bobojonova, said financial problems are often the cause of suicide in men, whereas among women the leading cause is domestic violence.

Men carry the responsibility of being the breadwinner and are expected to be able to provide for the family, "Society is used to seeing in a man a strong, brave person who takes care of his family."

But in times of economic crisis they struggle to fulfil this role and that can make them depressed, according to Bobojonova.

"They are not supposed to cry or show weakness. They have nowhere to turn and that is why they may take such a radical step," she said.

Six suicide cases in the last month involved unemployed men aged between 22 and 60, the local interior ministry office said.

Mental Illness as a Factor

Commenting on suicide statistics, the coordinator of the crisis centre Gulrukhsor, Mavzuna Hokimboeva, said there is a widespread perception—and law enforcement bodies are no exception—that suicide is linked with mental illness.

"According to our information, to a large extent it is financial difficulties in the family that lead to the rise in this phenomenon," Hokimboeva said.

Medical doctor Malika Saidalieva said that psychological illnesses tend to emerge against the backdrop of various factors including financial problems, "This could be the loss of a loved one, losing a job and a number of other reasons."

There is a widespread perception—and law enforcement bodies are no exception—that suicide is linked with mental illness.

She explained how the economic hardship could lead to suicidal thoughts, "Constant stress, a weakened immune system and nervous breakdown will lead to neurasthenia. [This brings] persistent thoughts including a desire to commit suicide."

Neurasthenia is a condition whose symptoms include fatigue, anxiety and depression.

Finding Hope

A 45-year-old resident of Khujand who gave his name as Samad told IWPR how he was driven to the brink of suicide when he lost his job.

He tried to find work but failed to get a stable job and earnings from temporary work were meagre. In his desperation, Samad turned to alcohol. He and his wife quarrelled constantly.

"I was ready to take my own life and even pictured in my mind how to do it. But one evening my youngest daughter sat on my lap and said, 'Daddy, I love you very much'," he said. "I felt reborn and realised that there are more important things than one's own worries."

The Issue of Loans

The decline in remittances puts a strain on people who have used funds sent by family members working as labour migrants as collateral to take out loans. Microcredit organisations accept a bank's letter confirming monthly transfers from a relative abroad as a guarantee for repayment.

The head of crime prevention among minors and young people at the interior ministry, Lieutenant-Colonel Rahimjon Abduvaliev, told IWPR that this year's suicide statistics included cases of men who took their own lives because they had problems repaying a loan. He was not able to give the number.

Barbara Kreuter, a consultant with the German Development Service advising the Tajik Association of Microfinance Organisations, confirmed that many people are struggling with loan repayments.

"This year delays in repayments have risen four times compared to 2008," she said.

Addressing the Crisis

The rise in suicides has been noted in the Soghd region over the last couple of years but the latest increase in attempts has attracted the authorities' attention.

The local government in the northern region of Soghd last month [July 2009] decided to set up a special commission to work on how to prevent suicide attempts.

The head of the department for social and cultural affairs and interethnic relations in the city administration of Khujand, Zulfia Umarova, said the commission plans to organise meetings and talks. Members of the commission will include a deputy of the Tajik parliament, a psychologist, a cleric, a police officer and a writer.

The administration is enlisting the help of mosque leaders.

"They will be asked to talk in their sermons about being patient and thinking of responsibility towards the family," Umarova said.

Tajik Women Have a High Suicide Rate Because of Domestic Violence

Mukammal Odinaeva

In the following viewpoint, Mukammal Odinaeva claims the high suicide rate of Tajik women can be attributed to widespread and unchecked domestic violence in the country and a lack of outreach for affected women. Odinaeva reports that legislation is being drafted to address the problem of domestic violence, but argues that there needs to be a cultural shift before it becomes acceptable for Tajik women to stand up for their rights. Odinaeva is a reporter for the Institute for War & Peace Reporting.

As you read, consider the following questions:

1. From January–September 2008, how many cases of female suicide were there in Tajikistan, as reported by the author?

2. According to Odinaeva, what is the most common method of suicide for Tajik women?

3. What are a few of the measures human rights activists are pressing for in Tajikistan to address the problem of female suicide, according to the author?

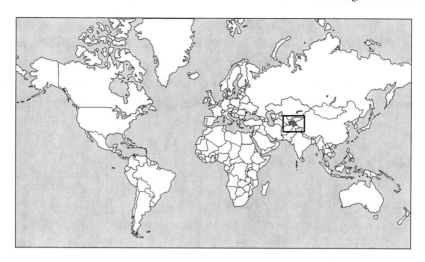

"One winter evening I went out into the yard, poured aviation fuel over my legs and set fire to myself," said Mosharif, a young Tajik woman from Vakhsh in eastern Tajikistan.

She was taken to hospital and survived, but she regrets that she did.

"Why did they save me? I don't want to live like this," she said.

Suicide rates are high among Tajik women because of unchecked domestic abuse and because victims are unaware of their rights.

Suicide rates are high among Tajik women because of unchecked domestic abuse and because victims are unaware of their rights.

An Epidemic of Suicide

From January to September 2008, the latest period for which statistics are available, there were 240 recorded cases of female suicide in Tajikistan. Experts think the true figures are a lot higher as some deaths are misreported.

"Suicide among women has become an epidemic, like HIV/ AIDS or malaria," said Mahmadullo Davlatov, a member of the Association of Psychologists of Tajikistan.

Human rights activists say around eight out of ten violent crimes occur within the family home. It is common for men to assault their wives, who enjoy little protection from relatives as they generally move to the husband's family home after marriage.

"Although there are no official figures on [the number of] victims of domestic violence, it's a very acute problem in Tajikistan and represents a great threat not just to women, but to the well-being of the whole of society," said Zebo Sharifova, executive director of the League of Women Lawyers.

Womens' rights groups list many reasons why women take such extreme measures—domestic violence, sexual assault, a husband's adultery, or the arrival of a second wife—polygamy is technically illegal but is common in Tajikistan. Other factors include lack of money, and the absence of a husband, leaving wives vulnerable to abuse from his relatives.

The Stress and Pain of Limited Options

Alternatives such as leaving are frequently not an option. A stigma attaches to women who seek a divorce, and their own families may be reluctant to take them back.

Fundamentally, says Orzu Ghanieva, who heads Gulrukhsor, a women's centre in the northern city of Khujand, suicide is a consequence of women being treated as "chattels and servants".

After she got married at just 16, Mosharif says her husband and mother-in-law beat her regularly, even when she was pregnant.

"I thought everything would change when my daughter was born, but it got even worse," she recalled. "My husband hit both me and the baby. He said I should get out of the house because I hadn't been able to bear him a son and he didn't need a daughter. At the age of 17 I no longer wanted to live. I kept thinking about how to be free of this nightmare. I dreamed of jumping in the river or setting myself on fire."

Methods of Suicide

As in Mosharif's case, one of the most common methods of suicide among women in Tajikistan—as in neighbouring Uzbekistan and Afghanistan—is self-immolation.

Some experts like Zafar Saidzod, formerly head of the Khovar news agency and now a presidential adviser, say self-immolation has deep roots that predate the advent of Islam and may be connected with older Zoroastrian beliefs.

"The preference for this specific method of [suicide in that] society is principally connected with the cult of fire," he said. "Fire is believed to cleanse the soul and end moral suffering."

Not all suicide cases involve young women. Sayram was married for 14 years and had four children before she made a number of suicide attempts—poisoning herself, throwing herself in a river, trying to hang herself, and cutting veins.

She was driven to desperation by her husband, who beat her badly and never gave her money for basics like food and children's clothing.

"In the end I lost sight of the sense of living," she recalled.

Eventually she doused herself in kerosene and set fire to herself. When she woke up in hospital she had 50 per cent burns.

A Lack of Legal Options

In other cases, women are driven to make a suicide attempt by members of their own families.

"I am the only girl in the family," said one young woman. "From the age of 12 I had a job as a cleaner and I was saving up so I could study to be a lawyer. But my brother forbade me from studying. He used to kick me and tell me not to go out of the house so I could remain as the servant to all of them.

From a legal point of view the problem, say many experts, is that Tajikistan lacks specific legislation concerning domestic violence.

She too set herself on fire. "I didn't want to die; I just wanted him to stop assaulting me."

From a legal point of view the problem, say many experts, is that Tajikistan lacks specific legislation concerning domestic violence. Cases can be brought under laws on common assault, but women are often afraid to go to the police because they do not believe they will get a fair hearing.

There is also the specific offence of "driving to suicide", under which 30 prosecutions took place in January–October last year.

Young wives are often mistreated by their in-laws, who regard them as little more than a source of free physical labour for the household.

Improvements Are Under Way

Lawyer Faizinisso Vohidova says the courts are increasingly prepared to handle domestic cases of this kind, and a number of women have been convicted of abusing their daughters-in-law.

In terms of legislation, the situation is not without hope, as a bill on domestic violence is currently being drafted.

Representatives of the public order department of the Ministry of Internal Affairs, meanwhile, told IWPR [Institute for War & Peace Reporting] that an internal order has been issued setting out penalties for police who fail to respond to complaints from allegations of domestic violence made by members of the public.

Tajik Women's Groups Press for Domestic Violence Law

Tajik women's groups are lobbying hard for a draft bill to protect families from violence, claiming a growing number of suicides among women can be blamed on the phenomenon. Though few would dispute that discrimination and violence against women are endemic in Tajikistan, the law has yet to acknowledge the problem exists. There is no legal concept of "violence within the family", and this creates a climate of impunity among offenders, experts say.

Mukammal Odinaeva and Nafisa Pisarejeva,
"Tajik Women's Groups Press for Domestic Violence Law,"
Institute for War & Peace Reporting, December 19, 2007.

A Cult of Secrecy

However, it is common for women not to take cases forward.

As academic Abdulvohid Shamolov explains, in Tajikistan one does not discuss one's domestic troubles with friends and relatives, let alone with outsiders.

"People frequently condemn women whose husbands assault and humiliate them," he said. "There's a perception they allow themselves to be treated like that. And crimes committed within the family remain invisible, and therefore go unpunished."

Dr Shoira Yusupova, a surgeon at Tajikistan's national burns centre, says it is common for husbands to get their wives to sign a statement that their burns were accidental.

Both Sayram and Mosharif recalled how their husbands visited them in hospital for this purpose.

"He asked me to tell the prosecutor the burns resulted from carelessness," said Mosharif. "I refused to do so for a long time, but he and his mother were always pressuring me. In the end I told the police it was an accident. Then my husband ran off to Russia."

The Case of Shamsia

IWPR spoke to one woman, Shamsia, whose husband was eventually convicted even though she did not report him herself.

Shamsia ended up in hospital after swallowing over 100 sharp items—broken razors, needles, nails and fragments of glass.

The marriage was an arranged one, and although she repeatedly returned to her parents' home after her husband attacked her, they always sent her back.

Doctors incorrectly diagnosed a stomach ulcer, and Shamsia's husband refused to pay for further investigation. He sent her back to her parents, where her father had her hospitalised again.

At that point she confided in a female relative, who informed the hospital authorities.

Shamsia's life was saved by an operation, and her husband was arrested, tried and convicted of forcing her to swallow the sharp objects.

The Government's Role

Experts say the government should be doing more to confront the problem of female suicide. It is the role of the state, said Ghanieva, to guarantee equal rights.

Among the measures human rights activists are pressing for are the domestic violence legislation currently in the drafting stage, a new commission which would work to prevent female suicide, and a network of social services to help women in difficulties.

Shamolov says that for a start, the authorities should set up a research centre to collate and study data on violence within the family so that the basic information is available.

Pessimists argue that since society is male-dominated there is little sense of the urgency of change.

Resources Are Needed to Address the Problem

A senior government official, speaking on condition of anonymity, told IWPR there was an awareness of the link between suicide and domestic violence. The reason why little was being done about it was not indifference, but lack of available funds, he said.

"The government has almost no funds for addressing domestic violence," he said. "And there are no statistics on it. We are under an obligation to gather data, but we don't get any resources allocated for this. So no one talks about it."

Dr Yusupova says the consequences of suicide attempts are far-reaching for the women involved and for those around them.

Treatment and recovery from appalling burn injuries are slow and painful for the victim.

"To see it is to experience physical and psychological pain," she said Dr Yusupova. "You wouldn't wish it on your worst enemy."

A French Company Is Plagued by a Spate of Suicides

Emma Charlton

In the following viewpoint, Emma Charlton documents the controversy over a series of suicides at France Telecom that experts believe illuminates the high stress and often tense relations between workers and corporate management in many French companies. Charlton explores the darker side to corporate culture, which is exacerbated by a shift to a more market-driven approach, and the alienating effect it is having on workers. Charlton is a reporter for Agence France-Presse.

As you read, consider the following questions:

1. How many suicides were there at France Telecom in a twenty-month period from 2008–2009, according to the author?

2. According to a survey by IMD, where does France rate in a group of fifty countries when it comes to the quality of worker-management relations?

3. According to the author, what is the suicide rate in France?

Short work weeks, enviably long lunches and vacations their American or Japanese counterparts can only dream of: French labour conditions are well known to be among the most generous in the world.

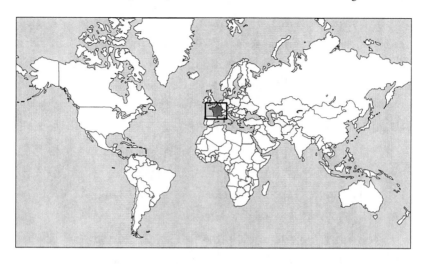

But a string of suicides at France Telecom has cast the spotlight on a darker side of French corporate life, where high stress and fraught relations with management drive many workers into depression.

A Much Bigger Problem

Statistically, it is not clear whether the 24 suicides and 14 attempted suicides at the former state-owned giant these past 20 months [2008–2009] are significant.

But for Jean-Claude Delgenes, whose consultancy Technologia is advising France Telecom following the deaths, they are "a symptom of a wider pollution" in French corporate culture.

"A lot of people identify with the France Telecom case," he said.

The group, which trades internationally as Orange, has undergone major restructuring as it opens up to competition, which unions say has left workers stressed and demoralised.

Thirty-two-year-old Stephanie e-mailed her father moments before jumping from her fourth-floor window at the firm last month [September 2009], saying: "I can't accept the new reorganisation in my department. I'm getting a new boss and I'd rather die."

"It happened when they told me I was good for nothing," said Yonnel Dervin, a 49-year-old telecoms technician who survived after stabbing himself in the stomach in a meeting last month. "I couldn't take any more."

A Callous Corporate Culture

As France shifts from a paternalist corporate culture to a flexible, market-driven one—symbolised by an invasion of US-style jargon such as "le deadline" or "le benchmarking"—workers are being left by the roadside.

"You only have to look outside France to realise there are happier places to work," Thomas Philippon, a French economist at New York's Stern business school, said in an interview published this week.

As France shifts from a paternalist corporate culture to a flexible, market-driven one—symbolised by an invasion of US-style jargon such as "le deadline" or "le benchmarking"—workers are being left by the roadside.

"In France there is a suspicion between hierarchical levels that does not exist elsewhere, or nowhere near as much."

An annual survey on the quality of worker-management relations in more than 50 countries, carried out by the Swiss business school IMD, regularly rates France in the bottom five.

One reason for this, Delgenes argues, is that France's system for recruiting managers—with a cast of business school graduates parachuted in at the top of companies—has led to a top-down, authoritarian management style.

"Compared to Germany, where you have managers who know a company from the inside, the training of our managers is deeply elitist," argued Delgenes.

Next-Desk Rivals

Some of the blame for the tension inside French companies rests with an educational system that churns out technocrats incapable of leadership and teamwork, says William Dab, France's former director general of health, the country's equivalent of the U.S. surgeon general. In 2008, Dab wrote a government-commissioned report recommending that health management play a central role in business school programs.

"Our chief executives come out of a school system based on individual competition," says Dab, now a professor at the Pasteur-Cnam School of Public Health in Paris. "They're the product of 10 years of education where it's been drilled into them that the guy at the desk next to them is a rival."

Richard Tomlinson and Gregory Viscusi,
"Suicides Inside France Telecom Prompting Sarkozy Stress Testing,"
Bloomberg Businessweek, January 25, 2010.

He cites the case of one French corporation, which had a canteen for senior management and another for common workers—a sure source of friction in a country with a tradition of republican equality.

Add to this a deep mistrust between business leaders, unions and the French state, dating back to the social struggles of the 19th century, and you have the ingredients for a corporate nightmare, Philippon argues.

Poor Management-Worker Communication

A TNS Sofres study published in the *Nouvel Observateur* magazine this week [in October 2009] showed only one-third of French workers feel well informed about goings-on at their firm—compared to two-thirds of Americans.

Asked how they felt about their firm, one-third said "disappointed", "suspicious" and "weary"—much higher than in Germany or the United States.

Most of the France Telecom suicides were lifelong civil servants struggling to adapt to a new market-oriented culture.

But suicides have also hit other large French groups, from carmakers Renault and Peugeot to energy giant Électricité de France, raising questions over whether bosses are driving their employees too hard.

Despite a statutory 35-hour working week, many French actually toil much longer with an hourly productivity that is among the highest in the developed world, according to the OECD [Organisation for Economic Co-operation and Development].

Most of the France Telecom suicides were lifelong civil servants struggling to adapt to a new market-oriented culture.

While repetitive strain injuries are on the decline in Britain and the United States, in France they have been multiplied by four in a decade.

To make matters worse, high unemployment and rigid hiring and firing practices mean French workers are less likely to leave an unhappy but safe job.

"People rarely move between companies, and the place of the public sector is traditionally strong. People are attached to their home region and job postings are usually enforced, rarely sought after," Delgenes said.

Suicide Rates in France

France has one of the highest suicide rates among the world's leading economies—at 17.6 per 100,000 compared to 13 in neighbouring Germany, 11 in the United States and 6.7 in

Britain, according to World Health Organization figures for 2005. Only Japan is higher at 24.2 per 100,000.

Officially, just under five percent of all French suicides are work related. According to Delgenes, the real figure is much higher, especially at a time of economic crisis.

"People are moved to jobs they are not properly trained for, so they make mistakes, and little by little they are marked as black sheep. They are pushed into a situation of failure."

Delgenes says France has a poor record on retraining people who lose their jobs in a lay-off plan. "That is a high-risk factor because people stay stuck in miserable situations."

The annual rate of suicide at France Telecom, at 16 per 100,000 people, is roughly the same as the general French population.

Looked at more closely, however, it is less than half the rate of 40 per 100,000 found among 45- to 55-year-old men, who make up most of the deaths.

And yet a disproportionate number killed themselves at their workplace or left letters blaming work for their despair, most recently a father of two who jumped from a highway overpass last week.

Bowing to pressure from public opinion, France Telecom's deputy chief executive Louis-Pierre Wenes, architect of the modernisation drive blamed for the suicides, resigned on Monday.

A Chinese Company Reports a Rash of Suicides

Wieland Wagner

In the following viewpoint, Wieland Wagner examines a rash of recent suicides at a sprawling Foxconn factory complex in Shenzhen, China, that has been attributed to the rigid regulations at the factory, the harsh work schedule, and the unsociable culture on the factory floor and in the corporate village. Wagner reports that the deaths have sparked criticism from outside and inside China, prompting the company to take steps to address the issue. Wagner is a reporter for Der Spiegel.

As you read, consider the following questions:

1. As reported by the author, how many people work at the Foxconn factory in Shenzhen?
2. How many suicides have there been from January–May of 2010, according to Wagner?
3. According to the author, what did a recent video released on the Chinese Internet show about Foxconn security guards?

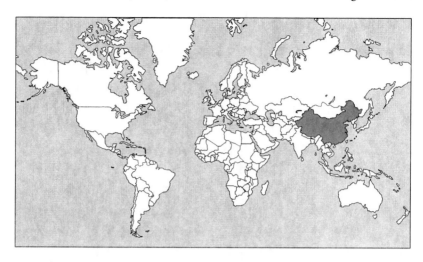

It's shortly after seven in the morning, a half-hour before the morning shift. Young Chinese workers file past gray-uniformed guards, pressing their corporate IDs on the electronic gates and waiting for the green light. Then they hurry through the labyrinth of the gray factory halls and workers' dorms.

Around 300,000 people work here in the southern Chinese city of Shenzhen, outside Hong Kong, on a gigantic factory complex belonging to the Taiwanese firm Foxconn. Another 120,000 people work at a smaller complex several streets away. They build cult products for global digital brands like Apple, Nintendo and Dell, ranging from the iPhone and iPad to the Notebook. Many sacrifice their health; others, even their lives.

Ma Xiangqian, 18, was part of this peculiar Foxconn world, where everything is numbered: buildings, machines, component parts, finished products and, of course, people. For wages of up to 1,940 yuan per month (€230, or $285), the young man from Henan province spent his 12-hour shifts shoving plastic pieces into a machine that formed casings for Apple computers. Then he went home to sleep with nine colleagues in a room of one of the many dormitory blocks on the factory complex.

Factory or "Campus"?

One morning in January [2010] Ma lay dead near the base of one of those buildings. Official cause of death: "Fall from a height." A total of 13 similar cases at Foxconn factories this year—10 leading to deaths—have produced similar findings. The latest death, on May 26, occurred hours after a personal visit to the factory by Terry Gou, who runs Foxconn's parent company. And in July 2009, a technician jumped to his death after coming under suspicion of stealing an iPhone prototype.

The series of apparent or attempted suicides has shaken the management of China's largest electronics manufacturer. Liu Kun, 40, who calls himself the director of media relations, goes around in a sweat-soaked shirt. He avoids the word "factory," preferring the word "campus"—as if Foxconn were a university. In a battery-driven golf cart—steered by Chen Hongfang, second in command at the company union, which is controlled by the Communist Party—Liu shows a visitor around the palm-lined streets. They want to prove how good the workers have it.

Liu points proudly at all the shops. Fast-food chains have franchises here; the Foxconn village has a factory hospital, where workers can walk in for treatment; there's a football stadium, a fitness center, a number of Internet cafés, a rehearsal room for the corporate dance troupe and a kind of academy. Television monitors installed along the streets—or in the cafeterias—play a corporate TV channel.

The series of apparent or attempted suicides has shaken the management of China's largest electronics manufacturer.

These opportunities for diversion don't change the fact that Foxconn workers have to spend their lives almost entirely on the complex. One cargo truck after another delivers components and carries away finished products. There are no warehouses at Foxconn. Once workers assemble a mobile phone or a laptop, the device goes straight to customers. This flow of products can't slow down. On Foxconn streets, workers are allowed to walk alongside each other only in pairs. If there are three of them, they must form a line.

Fastidious Regulations

Order and organization are everything, even in the factory kitchen. The gray building, from the outside, looks as boxlike and anonymous as the others, and the setting is industrial on the inside as well. An army of cooks in white smocks and rubber shoes prepares meals for the workers, overseen by Foxconn managers on a huge wall of monitors. There is fastidious regulation at every level, including the supply of ingredients, the dishwashing, the frying, baking, and boiling. Every day the cooks prepare three tons of pork, three tons of chicken, 60,000 eggs and 20 tons of rice.

Whether the sheer magnitude of the factory overwhelms the workers' psyches is not a question Foxconn managers are prepared to answer.

If you want to leave the kitchen, you have to wash your hands. Only then does the door open. Even in the gray, five-to-12-story dormitories, the workers have to press IDs on control devices before they can go outside.

Whether the sheer magnitude of the factory overwhelms the workers' psyches is not a question Foxconn managers are prepared to answer. Size, after all, guarantees low overhead and high profits—at least according to Steve Chu, 49, a Taiwanese man in charge of one of the multistory factory buildings. Nine-hundred workers labor on one floor alone.

The men and women in white uniform coats and bonnets are forbidden from holding personal conversations. This rule is printed on the flip side of their corporate IDs. The only sound is a whistle and hiss from the machines where they push green circuit boards for laptops or credit-card readers. On eight different conveyor belts they finish work on eight different products for several different world markets.

"The Devil Is in the Detail!"

Manager Chu and his assembly-line overseers spur the workers on, indefatigably, to be more efficient and precise. Even the steps of the stairwells have been garnished with warning phrases: "The devil is in the details!" Or, "Opportunity waits for those who are prepared!"

The motivational maxims are inspired by Terry Gou, the 59-year-old founder manager of Hon Hai Precision Industry, which owns Foxconn. Workers have adopted the respectful nickname "Lao Gou" (or "old Gou") for the charismatic but press-shy billionaire. His family fled China's communists, heading to Taiwan in 1949.

He built his empire 36 years ago with a factory for channel-changing dials on black and white TVs. Part of his $7,500 initial capital was borrowed from his mother. Later he manufactured connecting sockets for computers, and in 1988 he opened his first low-wage factory in mainland China.

But the recent spate of deaths and serious injuries have sparked criticism even from within China, and doubts have swirled about how the firm makes its cutting-edge electronic products.

Now Foxconn, along with other Taiwanese giants, supplies huge sectors of the electronics industry. Sometimes they manufacture mobile phones and laptops for global brands. Foxconn employs 800,000 people in the whole of China. In the spring it boosted its workforce, hiring 150,000 more workers.

A Generational Shift

Sociologists and other academics see the deaths as extreme signals of a more pervasive trend: a generation of workers rejecting the regimented hardships their predecessors endured as the cheap labor army behind China's economic miracle.

Rather than take their own lives, many more workers at Foxconn—tens of thousands more—have simply quit.

David Barboza,
"After Suicides, Scrutiny of China's Grim Factories,
New York Times, June 6, 2010.

But the recent spate of deaths and serious injuries have sparked criticism even from within China, and doubts have swirled about how the firm makes its cutting-edge electronic products. The family of the dead Ma Xiangqian aims to bring Foxconn to court to explain the deaths of its workers.

Brutal Torment

It is a battle of unequals. At the start of the year, Ma Zishan 58, and his wife Gao Chaoyin, 49, grew trees. Now they share a room near the Foxconn factory with two of their three daughters. They sleep on straw mattresses. The only wall decoration is a picture of their dead son, who, in keeping with Confucian tradition, bore the family's future hopes. "Foxconn, tell us the truth," the father has written in dark letters around the edge of the photo. "My life has lost its meaning," he says.

And his youngest daughter, Liqun, 22, and her boyfriend also worked at Foxconn until recently. They gave up their jobs to battle the Taiwanese factory colossus.

Liqun last saw her brother six days before he died. "He was upbeat," she says, "because he had just resigned." She adds that a production manager had brutally tormented him after a drilling fixture broke on his machine. As a punishment, Xiangqian had to clean the toilet.

Leaned up against the walls of their room stand placards used by the family to protest outside the Foxconn factory gates. With enlarged photos of Xiangqian's corpse, they want to draw attention to the inconsistencies in the story of his death. His sister Liqun tells of wounds she found on the head of his corpse—which looked like they had been made by a drill fixture. She also found strange injuries on his upper body, wounds which would not suggest suicide. Sections of Foxconn's surveillance video are missing from around the time of their worker's death.

"Illness of the Spirit"

Ma and his daughters speak cautiously, and seem shy. They avoid blaming the powerful Foxconn directly, but they insist the situation must be clarified. They want to challenge the official report of his death in court.

But factory spokesman Liu reacts indignantly to inquiries about the Ma case. He seems satisfied with the official autopsy report. "Who do you believe?" he asks. "Foxconn or the Ma family?"

He adds that Foxconn workers never have to clean toilets—after all, factory cleaners do that. Of course, there may be tragic incidents affecting the company's 420,000 workers in Shenzhen, he says. People suffer personal problems, heartache, homesickness, unfamiliar food flavors. "Or illnesses of the spirit," Liu says, raising his finger. One worker who recently threw himself off the balcony suffered from a persecution complex, he says, adding that the current workforce, who are mostly just over 20, are more vulnerable than that of previous generations.

Terry Gou's visit this week [in May 2010] failed to quell criticism. He denied the recent deaths were due to Foxconn working conditions. Hours later, a 23-year-old laborer in a different Foxconn complex, in northwestern China, dropped to his death from a dorm. And on Thursday, a 25-year-old man reportedly attempted suicide by cutting himself. He survived.

International Pressure?

A storm was ignited by a recent video released on the Chinese Internet, allegedly showing security guards at a Foxconn factory in Beijing kicking and hitting workers. Wang Tongxin, a Chinese trade union official, has warned that the supplier has to show more respect for the young Chinese people who work there. Following the death of the iPhone technician last year, Apple spoke out: "We demand that our suppliers treat their workers with respect and dignity."

Company spokesman Liu is thus keen to show visitors his factory's "mental health" center. A therapist gives advice to a worker, and red banners adorn facades of some of the dormitories, encouraging people to look after each other.

But within the residential buildings, workers continue their lives according to the logic of low-cost production. In rooms filled with 10 beds, half the residents lie exhausted on their mattresses. Some of those who find it too cramped here are stretched out in front of the televisions which hang in every stairway. Every break is precious: Soon they have to return to their next 12-hour shift.

America Is Experiencing a Rash of Gay Teen Suicides

Naseem Rakha

In the following viewpoint, author and journalist Naseem Rakha contends that homophobic attitudes and laws are contributing to the recent epidemic of gay teen suicides in the United States. Rakha argues that anti-gay sentiments and policies must be changed to eliminate institutional discrimination and harassment of gay teens.

As you read, consider the following questions:

1. According to the author, what is "Don't Ask, Don't Tell"?
2. Between September–October of 2010, how many gay young people committed suicide in the United States, according to Rakha?
3. According to a Gay, Lesbian and Straight Education Network survey, what percentage of gay, lesbian, bisexual and transgender kids are bullied in school in the United States, as reported by the author?

Don't ask, don't tell. This is the policy of the United States on homosexuals serving in the military. Don't ask a person if they identify themselves as lesbian, gay, bisexual, or transgender [LGBT], and certainly don't breathe a word about your sexuality if you happen to fit into one of those groups. If you do, expect to get kicked out.

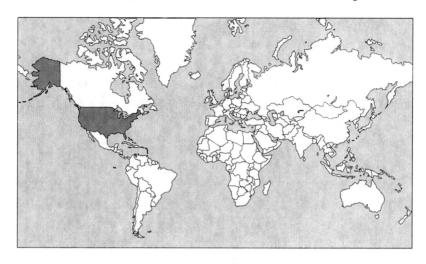

This isn't news. DADT [don't ask, don't tell] and its damning message have existed for more than a decade. What is new is that just last week [October 2010] the Obama administration indicated it would appeal a recent lower court decision to ban the law as unconstitutional. President Barack Obama wants Congress to repeal "don't ask, don't tell", keeping it out of the hands of the more conservative-leaning courts which, Obama believes, will ultimately uphold the law.

While the political and legal wrangling over DADT may be confusing, the law's message remains intact: "If you're queer, keep it to yourself."

This may be why, just days later, the president filmed a three-minute video asking LGBT teens to hang in there. "You are not alone," he tells them. "Things will get better."

The rash of suicides has drawn attention to some frightening facts about being gay in America.

An Epidemic of Gay Teen Suicides

President Obama's message is one of more than 5,000 that have sprung up on YouTube in the last few weeks in an attempt to combat what appears to be an epidemic of gay teen suicide in my country. Since September, at least five youths have taken their lives, all of them queer-identified, and all of them victims of harassment. These kids were taunted in school, beaten and shunned. One, an 18-year-old Rutgers' student, killed himself after a tryst was secretly filmed then dropped onto YouTube.

The rash of suicides has drawn attention to some frightening facts about being gay in America. According to a survey done by the Gay, Lesbian and Straight Education Network, almost 85% of LGBT kids are bullied in school. A Massachusetts Youth Risk Survey indicates that gay teens are four times more likely to attempt suicide than their straight peers, and a report out of the University of Pittsburgh Medical School reveals that LGBT teens are 190–400% more likely to become drug and alcohol addicted.

For some, like Oklahoma state representative Sally Kern, these statistics bare evidence to arguments against the LGBT "lifestyle". Homosexuality, according to Kern, is a deadly disease "akin to cancer . . . and more dangerous to the US then terrorism". "It is not an equal or valid option," says New York gubernatorial candidate Carl Paladino. And earlier this month, Boyd Packer, the second-highest-ranking authority of the Mormon Church, told more than a million viewers that LGBT children will not get better until they reject "unnatural and unholy" impulses that guide them toward same-sex relationships.

Homophobia Leads to Suicides

In light of these kinds of comments, and laws such as DADT, I have to wonder, is it being homosexual that is killing our children, as Kern and others suggest? Or is it homophobic attitudes and laws that make being identified as LGBT deadly?

Being gay in America is not like being black or Hispanic or Jewish or Muslim, or any other ethnic or religious group

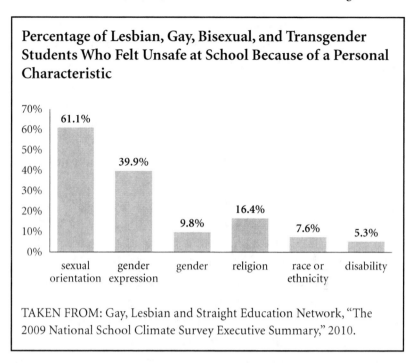

Percentage of Lesbian, Gay, Bisexual, and Transgender Students Who Felt Unsafe at School Because of a Personal Characteristic

TAKEN FROM: Gay, Lesbian and Straight Education Network, "The 2009 National School Climate Survey Executive Summary," 2010.

victimised by discrimination. Being a gay kid in my country is isolating. Most LGBT children do not have a community to turn to—let alone parents willing to accept their child's sexual orientation. Most churches don't accept that there is a biological basis for homosexuality; some go so far as to equate it with drug use and stealing. "Pray gay away" has become a catchphrase among the zealots who make their opinions known from Capitol Hill to our children's classrooms. One doesn't have to look long online to find the vitriol that so-called adults track into the homes—and minds—of kids trying to find their way.

More Acceptance and Tolerance Are Essential

Some say it is easier being gay in the US today than in the past, when even the topic of homosexuality remained in the closet. They point to TV shows like *Glee*, which features a young gay teen and his struggles against bullies. And it is true that, in some cities, the LGBT-identified have a greater sense of freedom and safety. But unlike the US's neighbours to the north and south, which have made it illegal to discriminate based on sexual orientation, the United States has no such federal protection; nor does the federal government recognise gay marriages. And, of course, there still remains "don't ask, don't tell".

To think that laws like DADT or the homophobic comments of political and religious leaders do not spawn fear, hate, hostility, and humiliation is not only ignorant, it is dangerous. Fortunately, their voices are not the only ones in the choir. The "It Gets Better" project has had over a million viewers since it was launched earlier this month. The various films are remarkable for their honesty and depth of emotion. They give a clear view into the realm of prejudice, and they lay blame precisely where it needs to be placed—on the adults who teach their children to hate, and on each person who condones the discrimination of homosexuals with a shrug of the shoulders, or worse, a belief that this discrimination is somehow moral.

In this day of "don't ask, don't tell", we must do its precise opposite. Ask why LGBT kids are killing themselves, and tell the truth about the reasons.

Indonesia's Poor Are Committing Suicide

Indra Swari

Indra Swari is a lecturer at Parahyangan Catholic University's School of Social and Political Sciences. In the following viewpoint, she discusses a rash of suicides in Indonesia apparently caused by financial difficulties and homelessness. Swari argues that poverty is so severe and widespread that it proves the Indonesian government has failed to meet the needs of its citizens on a fundamental level.

As you read, consider the following questions:

1. What is the suicide rate in Indonesia, according to Swari?
2. According to Émile Durkheim, what are the three types of suicide as reported by the author?
3. How does gender affect suicide rates, in the author's opinion?

On Aug. 13, 2010, the *Jakarta Post* printed a story about Khoir Umi Latifah, a 25-year-old woman who committed suicide and murdered her two sons by setting herself and her children on fire in Sleman regency, Yogyakarta—a tragedy allegedly resulting from depression caused by financial hardship.

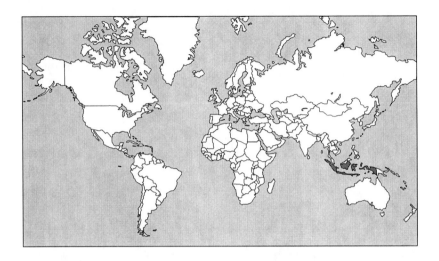

Umi worked as a housekeeper at a boarding house where she occupied a room with her husband, 30-year-old Slamet Yahya, and her two sons, Muhammad Lindu Aji, 4, and two-and-half-year-old Muhammad Dwi Arya Saputra.

According to the report, the incident took place while Umi's husband was not at home. She locked herself in a bathroom and poured gasoline over herself and her sons before igniting the fatal blaze.

A boarding house resident was unable to immediately assist them because of the locked door.

When the door was finally opened, Umi was found dead with severe burns all over her body. Her sons were rushed to the hospital but could not be saved. The youngest boy passed away first while the older son perished three hours later.

Economic Problems Lead to Suicide

Sadly, this is not the only case of poverty leading to suicide in Indonesia. In the last few months the mass media have reported several similar cases of poor people committing suicide because of financial difficulties.

According to the World Health Organization, the average annual rate of deaths by suicide in Indonesia is 24 per 100,000 people, many of which are attributed to poverty and homelessness.

Most people agree that suicide is a psychological phenomenon. Nonetheless, if suicidal tendencies are higher among a particular group of people—such as the poor—then suicide is not merely psychological, it is a sociological phenomenon as well.

Sociologist Émile Durkheim stated that the causes of suicide are often external rather than internal.

Three Kinds of Suicide

Based on Durkheim's sociological perspective, there are three types of suicide—egoistic, altruistic and anomic suicide.

Egoistic suicide is attributed to a person's inability to see any reason to continue living. It is the result of excessive "egoistic" individualism, where the individual ego asserts itself immoderately at the expense of the social ego.

Altruistic suicide stems from the conceptualization that the decision to end life is beyond life itself.

There are cases where persons kill themselves not because they believe it is their right to do so, but on the contrary, because it is their "duty".

This type of suicide explains cases in ancient times when women committed suicide by jumping onto their husbands' funeral pyres, symbolizing a woman's total devotion to her husband.

In fact, not all women committed this act voluntarily, but many had little faith in their future because they believed that there was no longer a place for them in society. So, frankly speaking, it was social pressure that actually killed them.

Anomic suicide relates to unbearable external pressures such as economic crisis, marital problems and academic or professional [concerns]. On the other hand, in some cases

Indonesia's Poverty Levels, 1990–2003		
Year	Numbers below the Poverty Level (millions)	% of Total Population
1990	27.2	15.1
1996	22.5	11.3
1999	47.9	23.4
2002	38.4	18.2
2003	37.3	17.4

TAKEN FROM: United Nations Environment Program, "Indonesia: Integrated Assessment of the Poverty Reduction Strategy Paper."

prosperity has also been blamed for suicide. In Durkheim's words, "Every disturbance of equilibrium, even though it may involve greater comfort and raising a general pace of life, provides an impulse to voluntary death".

For some people poverty becomes so unbearable it convinces them to end their life.

Gender and Suicide Rates

The economically driven suicide committed by Umi, and many others, falls under the category of anomic suicide, though they could also be related to the egoistic classification, as the two are closely linked.

This tragedy further demonstrates that the burden of poverty has reached alarming levels. For some people poverty becomes so unbearable it convinces them to end their life.

Clearly suicide is often related to social problems such as poverty and injustice, but gender inequality can also be another factor. I did not find statistics on the number of men and women who have committed suicide because of poverty. However from media reports I have observed that women are more likely to commit suicide than men, and like Umi, are more likely to intentionally kill their children before killing themselves.

This could relate to cultural norms, and patriarchal norms in particular, which assign women—regardless of their working status—responsibility for most domestic responsibilities, including managing household financial matters.

Women are also responsible for ensuring that food is always on the family table, regardless of economic circumstances. For some poor women these responsibilities lead to depression, and sometimes suicide.

Government's Culpability in the Crisis

At a macro level this is an indication that the government has failed to completely provide for the basic needs of its people, especially the poor.

The cases of suicide among the poor also mirror the complexity of poverty. Poverty is more than just numbers. It is a human tragedy.

Israel Must Protect Itself from Suicide Protests

Caroline B. Glick

In the following viewpoint, Caroline B. Glick scrutinizes the increasing use of suicide protests to discredit Israel and foment global opposition to Israeli policies. Glick argues that bureaucratic and political means should be utilized to counter this method and to damage the reputation of groups involved in suicide protests. Glick is a contributor to the Jerusalem Post.

As you read, consider the following questions:

1. According to Glick, what is the City of David project?
2. Who is Rachel Corrie, as reported by the author?
3. In the author's view, how are suicide protests criminal?

David Be'eri is either much admired or much hated, depending on how you feel about Israel and Jewish heritage. Be'eri is the founder and head of the Ir David Foundation, a nonprofit organization dedicated to excavating, preserving and developing biblical Jerusalem, the City of David.

The City of David Project

When Be'eri began his project in 1986, the City of David, located just opposite the Old City, was in shambles. Former excavations were hidden beneath heaps of garbage and debris.

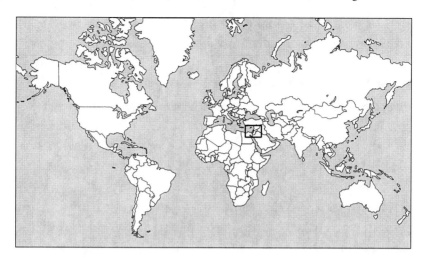

Owing to his efforts, today the City of David is one of Israel's most beloved tourist attractions. Some 500,000 tourists visit the site each year. Seventeen archaeological excavations have been undertaken there or are currently ongoing. Annual archaeological conferences at the site attract leading scholars from all over the world.

One of the keys to Be'eri's success has been the close relations he has cultivated with the local Arabs. Hundreds of local Arabs have worked in the City of David on the various excavations.

But in the past few months, and particularly since the [President Barack] Obama administration began pressuring Israel to curb its sovereignty in Jerusalem, things have begun to change. Leftist groups including Peace Now, Ir Amim, B'Tselem, the Association for Civil Rights in Israel, Rabbis for Human Rights, and Emek Shaveh have begun organizing frequent protests.

According to Udi Ragones, the spokesman for Ir David, the various leftist groups collaborate openly with two Arab groups that have been formed over the past year: Silwannet and the Wadi Hilweh Information Center. Peace Now's Hagit Ofran is often seen working with Jawad Sayam from the information center.

One of the information center's employees also works for Emek Shaveh, an organization of anti-Zionist archaeologists.

Protests Turn Violent

Over the past month [November–December 2010], what began as nonviolent protests against Ir David turned violent. A month ago anti-Israel activists set several cars ablaze. Local Arabs who work with the Ir David Foundation began receiving threats. The car of one such Arab was set on fire.

Two weeks ago, the demonstrations morphed into suicide protests as activists set up a roadblock in the middle of the street, ambushed an Ir David security guard and began violently attacking him. In order to fend off his attackers, the guard shot his pistol and killed one of them. Using faux footage, the protesters accused the guard of murder in cold blood. The police rejected the accusation. Channel 2 [a TV station in Israel] initially backed up the protesters' claim, but later its reporter recognized he had been used.

Last Friday, the violence was ratcheted up several notches when Be'eri was targeted by an ambush. As he drove to his home in Ir David with his 13-year-old son, the car in front of him suddenly hit the brakes.

Be'eri drove around the car and was greeted by an ambush of demonstrators who attacked him with stones.

Blocked from backing away by a car that had suddenly stopped, Be'eri had to decide between opening fire and driving through the protest. He drove through, hitting two of his attackers. Both were minors. Neither sustained serious injuries and were out and about within hours of the event.

The stone throwers were not the only people who participated in the ambush. Six or seven photographers and at least one employee of the Wadi Hilweh Information Center were also on the scene. The photographers hailed from the Far Left Hebrew-language Walla web portal and from several European media outlets. They filmed Be'eri running over his attackers from multiple angles. They then quickly sold the story to the world as a tale of a vicious "settler" who ran over two innocent children on their way home from the mosque, just because he is an evil settler.

An Ambush

But as Ragones notes, "We were actually lucky that the media were there. The photos that were supposed to frame Be'eri showed clearly that the whole thing was a setup."

Not only does the footage show that Be'eri was ambushed, it shows that the photographers were integral members of the ambush team. The children's role was to provoke Be'eri into killing or injuring them by attacking him with rocks. The photographers' role was to photograph the children getting killed or hurt.

The Ir David Foundation accuses the Wadi Hilweh Information Center of organizing the incident. The presence of the center's employees on the scene in the footage lends credence to the allegation. Ir David also argues that the entire episode was the product of close coordination between the information center and the leftist groups that work with it to demonize, discredit and otherwise harm Ir David specifically and Israeli control over unified Jerusalem generally.

The Rise of Suicide Protests

What is new about Friday's incident is not its nature, but its location. As Marc Prowissor, the director of security projects for the One Israel Fund, a nonprofit that supports stressed Jewish communities in Judea, Samaria, the Galilee and the Negev notes, these sorts of suicide protests have been going on for at least a decade.

Early incidents that had strategic impact on Israel's international standing were the Muhammad al-Dura affair in October 2000 and the Rachel Corrie incident in 2003. In the former, Palestinian security forces worked with a Palestinian cameraman and France 2 to cook up the libel accusing IDF [Israel Defense Forces] of killing the Palestinian boy Muhammad al-Dura. A French court ruled last year that the footage, which shows al-Dura moving after he allegedly died, was falsified.

In the second incident, Corrie was brought to Gaza by the non-Israeli International Solidarity Movement [ISM] and deployed to block IDF forces from carrying out counterterror operations. Corrie became the poster girl for suicide protesters when an IDF bulldozer operator, who could not see her, ran Corrie over as she sought to block his operations.

Growing Cooperation Between Leftists and Terrorists

Since 2000, there has been escalating cooperation between Israeli leftist organizations with foreign pro-jihad groups like ISM and Palestinian terror and political warfare outfits. This new cooperation first gained prominence as the Israeli group Anarchists Against the Wall began participating in the weekly Palestinian/ISM riots against IDF units at Bi'ilin and Na'alin in 2003.

Prowissor notes that throughout Judea and Samaria, especially around olive harvest season, Rabbis for Human Rights and like-minded radical groups bus Arab protesters into areas where they do not live to stir up and participate in protests.

"Their modus operandi is always the same," Prowissor explains. "They stage violent attacks in front of their own cameras with the aim of provoking local Israelis to defend themselves. For instance, they stone Jewish cars and if a Jewish driver gets out and tries to fend off his attackers, they film him and accuse him of attacking them for no reason."

The weekly protests at Bi'ilin and Na'alin involve Palestinian, Western and Israeli rioters attacking IDF forces and Border Police units with stones and Molotov cocktails.

Five months ago, the protesters began using the same tactics against Israeli civilians at Neveh Tzuf in the Binyamin region. A few weeks ago they added the Carmei Tzur community in Gush Etzion to their list of targets.

As for Jerusalem, the riots in Sheikh Jarrah every Friday have been going on for several months. They spread to Ir David on Friday.

Suicide Protests Are Effective Tools

The reason for this is clear enough. Suicide protests are an effective means of harming Israel. Just look at the Turkish terror ship *Mavi Marmara*. The nine suicide protesters onboard who were killed while attacking IDF naval commandos with knives, guns and bats are a bonanza for Israel's enemies. They are being used to drag Israel before the international hanging jury at the UN [United Nations], the Hague [home of the International Criminal Court], in US university campuses and throughout Europe.

What can be done about this growing menace? How can Israel defend itself against it? Suicide protests work on three levels simultaneously.

To neutralize their impact, Israeli citizens and officials have to develop strategies to contend with them on all three levels.

Suicide protests are an effective means of harming Israel.

Strategies to Address Suicide Protests

The most basic level is the criminal level. It is criminal to solicit violence. It is criminal to foment violence against citizens and security and police forces. It is criminal to conspire to carry out violence or impede soldiers, police and other security forces in the lawful dispatch of their duties.

Bearing this in mind, the police and the IDF should be directed to investigate all organizations suspected of planning, directing or participating in violent protests. When they get advance notice of protests, they can and should be preempted. It is legal for the police to arrest the protesters en route to illegal demonstrations.

Then too, cases should be built against sponsoring organizations. Groups instigating violence should be banned.

Suicide protests, like suicide bombs, use violence to advance political goals. In Israel's case, they are used to demonize the state and its citizens in a bid to coerce the government into acting in a manner that endangers it.

Bureaucratic and political tools should be employed to scuttle these efforts. For instance, in the aftermath of Friday's ambush in Ir David, the media watch group Tadmit sent a letter to the Government Press Office [GPO] requesting that it withdraw the press credentials from the photographers present at the scene. The GPO should act on Tadmit's request and deny or remove press credentials from any self-proclaimed reporter or photographer who participates in violent, illegal activities aimed against the state.

Suicide protests, like suicide bombs, use violence to advance political goals.

Beyond that, Israeli citizens' groups and the government should actively discredit groups involved in suicide protests. Data should be gathered against participating organizations and should be rapidly released every time an event like last Friday's ambush takes place.

Legal Aspects of Anti-Israel Strategy

Finally, there is the legal aspect of the suicide protest strategy. The alliance of Arab, Israeli and Western anti-Israel groups use suicide protests as a means of attacking Israel in foreign and international legal areas, like British courts and the Hague. Both private citizens and the government should sue local groups who collaborate with such initiatives for damages. To the extent that enabling legislation is required to bring such suits, the Knesset [Israeli legislature] should pass such legislation.

The local media initially ran the story of Be'eri's ambush just as the leftist-Arab coalition wanted them to. Be'eri was portrayed as an aggressive, violent settler who ran over two innocent Palestinian children for no reason. But then the suicide protesters overreached.

Suicide protests are the newest and, so far, most effective weapon in the political war against Israel.

On Sunday they ambushed and stoned a Channel 2 camera crew. Sunday night the truth was out.

But next time they will probably be more careful.

Suicide protests are the newest and, so far, most effective weapon in the political war against Israel. It is the task of the government and citizens alike to develop and implement strategies to blunt its effectiveness.

Periodical and Internet Sources Bibliography

The following articles have been selected to supplement the diverse views presented in this chapter.

Nick Amies	"Top Goalkeeper's Suicide Exposes Lonely, Complex World of Players with Problems," Deutsche Welle, November 12, 2009. www.dw-world.de.
Owen Bowcott	"Suicide Rate on the Rise, Figures Show," *Guardian*, January 28, 2010.
Chosun Ilbo	"Suicide's Impact Spreads Through Families," April 1, 2010.
Alina Dain	"Scientists Link Gene Mutations to Risk of Suicide," Deutsche Welle, February 5, 2010. www.dw-world.de.
Max Harrold	"Bullying Boosts Gay and Lesbian Suicide Rates," *Montreal Gazette*, February 3, 2011.
Institute for War & Peace Reporting	"Driven to Suicide," June 19, 2008. http://iwpr.net.
Henry McDonald	"Hairdressers in Northern Ireland to Be Trained to Spot Suicidal Clients," *Observer*, September 6, 2009.
Newsweek	"Killer Economy?" January 14, 2009.
Roger Pulvers	"Now Suicide Has Become a Political Issue, How Will Japan Address It?" *Japan Times*, September 20, 2009.
Ken Stier	"Suicides: Watching for a Recession Spike," *Time*, February 9, 2009.
Li Xing	"Debate: Chinese Mothers," *China Daily*, February 9, 2011.

GLOBALVIEWPOINTS

CHAPTER 4

Suicide as an Act of Terrorism

Israel Is Vulnerable to Suicide Bombers

Pierre Heumann

Pierre Heumann is the Middle East correspondent for the Swiss weekly magazine Weltwoche. *In the following viewpoint, he claims that border security between Egypt and Israel must be re-evaluated in the wake of the Dimona suicide bombing. Heumann notes that numerous gaps in security have allowed not only drug dealers and refugees to come in unchecked, but also the terrorist who perpetrated the Dimona attack.*

As you read, consider the following questions:

1. According to the author, how many people were killed in the Dimona attack?
2. Who was the terrorist responsible for the attack, as reported by Heumann?
3. According to the author, how long is the border between Israel and Egypt?

Terrorists struck again in Israel on Monday [February 4, 2008], in the first suicide bombing the country has seen in a year. It was an attack that politicians and military officers say they have seen coming for days. The bloody deed, which claimed the lives of one Israeli woman and the two suicide

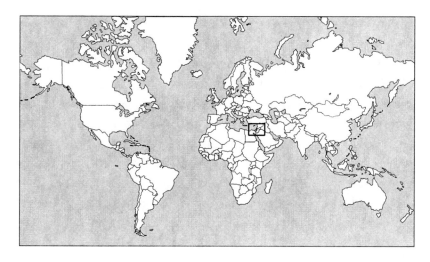

bombers, came as no surprise for many Israelis. Now that the border between the Gaza Strip and Egypt is open, it has become easier for terrorists to reach Israel from Gaza. Security experts have been warning that terrorists in Gaza would see this as a new opportunity—and would take advantage of it. This week, they were proven right.

Three organizations claimed responsibility for the attack in a shopping center in the southern Israeli city of Dimona. The first is the Popular Front for the Liberation of Palestine, which is fighting an uncompromising battle against Israel. The second is the previously unknown National Resistance Brigades, a group of former activists who consider Hamas [a Palestinian Islamic militant movement in the Gaza Strip] too moderate. Finally, the military wing of the Fatah Party says that it was involved in the suicide bombing.

Political Implications

This last claim is especially damaging to Palestinian President Mahmoud Abbas, who heads the Fatah Party and is in peace talks with Israeli Prime Minister Ehud Olmert. Abbas denies his supporters had anything to do with the attack, but Mussa

Arafat, the terrorist who was wearing the belt of explosives in Dimona, was a member of Fatah's military wing.

Abbas, who has condemned the attack, must now face questions (not for the first time) over whether he has his organization under control. Interestingly enough, the one organization that has not boasted about the attack is the radical Islamic group Hamas. Although a spokesman for Hamas praised the attack, calling it "justified," he also said that his organization was not involved. This reticence may have something to do with the fact that Hamas is eager not to create any new problems with Egypt. Cairo is concerned that the opening of the Gaza Strip toward Egypt could strengthen the Muslim Brotherhood within its own borders.

The suicide bomber, Mussa Arafat, who came from the southern Gaza Strip, had an easy time of it. He probably chose the route through Egypt to reach Israel. He was able to cross the border into Egypt in Rafah, where Palestinians bulldozed a border wall separating Egypt and Gaza a week and a half ago. This meant that Arafat could easily reach his real target, Israel, through the Sinai Peninsula. The border between Sinai, which is part of Egypt, and Israel is porous and mostly unguarded. After crossing into Israel's Negev Desert, Arafat had to travel only 100 kilometers (62 miles) to reach Dimona. It hasn't yet been determined whether he had local helpers for his trek to Dimona.

The nonchalance with which Israel has accepted the gaps in its border fence is astonishing.

Drug Dealers, Prostitutes, Refugees—and Terrorists

The nonchalance with which Israel has accepted the gaps in its border fence is astonishing. At the international airport in Tel Aviv, Israeli border agents question arriving passengers in painstaking detail before issuing entry visas, and the West Bank is being sealed off with a security fence. But at its border with Egypt, Israel tolerates "that anyone can get in who wants to get in," says Israeli Interior Minister Meir Sheetrit.

Israel's roughly 300-kilometer (186-mile) desert border with Egypt is not secured and in many places not even marked by a fence. Israeli intelligence is aware of at least 30 locations where it is possible to cross the border between the two countries without having to pass through a border control. Many of Israel's military observation posts are either permanently or often unmanned. This lack of security is attributable to successive administrations' unwillingness to pay the necessary costs of a fence that would run upwards of €500 million ($734 million), as Sheetrit estimates.

For years, the journey through the Sinai Desert—either on foot, on camelback or in SUVs [sport-utility vehicles]—has been the preferred route from Egypt into Israel for drug dealers, prostitutes and African refugees. Officials in Jerusalem now fear that terrorists will join the influx—and will come equipped with explosives.

In the wake of the Dimona bombing, Israeli hard-liners are calling for a large-scale military campaign against the Gaza Strip so that Israel can put a stop to the terrorists once and for all.

A Demand for Military Action in Gaza

The situation is more explosive than ever. In recent days, Egyptian security officials have arrested 15 armed Palestinians in the Sinai Peninsula, including 12 members of the radical Islamic Hamas organization. A short time earlier, the Egyptians apprehended two members of the Muslim Brotherhood who were carrying explosive belts. And in recent weeks authorities cracked another terrorist cell that was in possession of explosive materials.

THE SCHOOL OF TERROR...

"The School of Terror," cartoon by Karsten Schley, www.CartoonStock.com. Copyright © by Karsten Schley. Reproduction rights obtainable from www.CartoonStock.com.

Despite these successes, it may already be too late to avoid an escalation. In recent days, Palestinians have taken advantage of the open border to bring weapons and ammunition into the Gaza Strip, including armor-piercing grenades, rockets and antiaircraft missiles, Yuval Diskin, the head of Israel's domestic security agency, told the Israeli cabinet on Sunday. According to Diskin, dozens of Palestinian activists trained in Iranian camps have also returned to Gaza in recent days.

In the wake of the Dimona bombing, Israeli hard-liners are calling for a large-scale military campaign against the Gaza Strip so that Israel can put a stop to the terrorists once and for all. But a look into the annals of the Israeli military reveals that this wouldn't be the first time. Besides, there is no evidence that military force is even capable of solving the problem.

Gaza's Ghost Suicide Bombers Are Identified

Abdul Hameed Bakier

In the following viewpoint, Abdul Hameed Bakier reveals that recent investigations show the mysterious "ghost" suicide bombers who have been so effective against Israeli forces in Gaza belong to the military wing of the Izz ad-Din al-Qassam Brigades of Hamas. Bakier reports that the "ghost" bombers are carefully chosen and groomed from an early age and include females as well as males. Bakier is a reporter for the Jamestown Foundation.

As you read, consider the following questions:

1. As reported by the author, how many young people make up al-Qassam's battalions?
2. Who are the "Booby-Trapped Martyrs", according to Bakier?
3. According to the author, who is Mahmoud al-Rifi?

Recently, Islamic and jihadi Internet forums circulated an article entitled "The Ghost suicide bombers. Who are they? And how do they spend their day?" The posting, written by the Gaza correspondent for the influential Doha-based Islamonline website, included a short interview with the trainers of Hamas' [referring to the Palestinian Islamic militant movement in Gaza] suicide bombers.

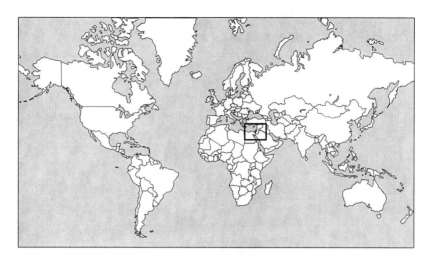

Who Are the Ghost Suicide Bombers?

Islamonline's correspondent, Muhammad al-Sawaf, said the suicide bombers, known as "Ghosts" to other Gaza militants, are the first line of defense in Gaza. They spend up to 48 hours at a time in ditches, reciting verses from the Quran while waiting for Israeli forces to pass by in order to blow them up. The bombers belong to the military wing of the Izz ad-Din al-Qassam [Brigades] battalions of Hamas. Abu Moath, an al-Qassam leader supervising the suicide bombers, said the bombers are very determined individuals chosen carefully by Hamas: "They live like any other pious Palestinian youth. Some of them are university students that go about their lives without raising unwanted attention or bragging about their end mission. They go through a special faith program."

Since the start of the conflict in Gaza, the "ghost" suicide bombers have isolated themselves from families and friends. They spend their time hidden close to areas where Israeli forces deploy. On the selection criteria for suicide bombers, Abu Moath briefly explained that only young people are chosen from the ranks of al-Qassam's battalions, which number up to ten thousand fighters. Abu Moath disclosed females are also recruited to the ranks of the suicide bombers. The candi-

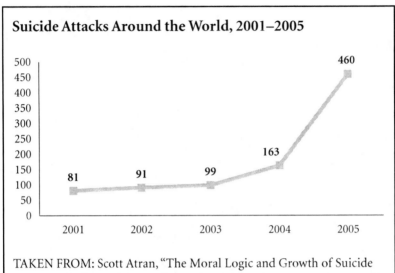

Suicide Attacks Around the World, 2001–2005

TAKEN FROM: Scott Atran, "The Moral Logic and Growth of Suicide Terrorism," *The Washington Quarterly*, Spring 2006.

date bombers are secretly scrutinized by al-Qassam lieutenants to make sure they are religiously committed and responsible. The next phase is to notify the bomber of their acceptance and put them through psychological and military training on weapons and tactics, especially those used by the Israel Defense Forces (IDF). Abu Moath asserts that all through the selection and training phases the suicide bombers are tutored by religious clerics and Islamic preachers. Upon completion of training, the bombers are sent behind enemy lines. Each group of suicide bombers is compartmentalized and does not know the location or composition of other groups to avoid compromising their comrades if one of them is captured by the Israelis. Abu Moath admits such captures happen very often because the suicide bombers operate behind enemy lines. Each suicide bomber is issued special weapons and a custom-tailored explosive belt.

The "Booby-Trapped Martyrs"

Other Hamas units of suicide bombers include the "Booby-Trapped Martyrs." These martyr units are designed to deploy on the streets and alleys of Gaza's cities, armed with heavier explosive belts than those used by the "ghosts." These units are as secret and compartmentalized as the "ghost" suicide bombers and deploy with Hamas commando units tasked with kidnapping Israeli soldiers.

Many forum chatters hailed and prayed for the "ghost" and "martyr" suicide bombers, posting comments such as: "It is only my lack of luck that I am not with them. I wish them all the best in this life and hereafter. May God give them steadfastness and determination, amen."

In another interview by Islamonline correspondent al-Sawaf, al-Qassam Brigades spokesman Abu Obeida said Hamas fighters have surprised the Israeli forces with offensive attacks rather than the expected defensive operations. He said the suicide bomber Mahmoud al-Rifi, whom he claimed stayed for days in a ditch on the al-Raes mountain west of Gaza city and blew up an Israeli commando unit, was one example of Hamas' successful new guerilla warfare tactics. However, other sources said al-Rifi did not carry out a suicide attack; rather, he waited for Israeli forces in a ditch on the al-Raes mountain and attacked a detachment of Israeli commandos with a machine gun, killing two Israeli soldiers before being killed while trying to take a third injured soldier prisoner.

Even though Hamas has enough experience and possible accomplices among Palestinians living in Israel to resume suicide attacks in Israeli cities, Israeli forces demonstrated their ability to prevent suicide attacks in the assault on Gaza.

Attacks Expected to Resume Soon

According to earlier threats by Hamas leaders, Hamas is expected to resume suicide bombing attacks in Israeli cities in retaliation for the war on Gaza. Regardless of the Israeli wall built to prevent suicide bombers from entering Israel, Hamas leaders allege they have managed to infiltrate tens of their suicide bombers who are already in place in Israel and the West Bank awaiting orders. Even though Hamas has enough experience and possible accomplices among Palestinians living in Israel to resume suicide attacks in Israeli cities, Israeli forces demonstrated their ability to prevent suicide attacks in the assault on Gaza. The absence of successful suicide attacks on Israeli forces in the conflict is likely an indication of Hamas' inability to recruit enough volunteers to perpetrate suicide bombings, regardless of whatever claims are made by the Hamas leadership.

Iraq Is Torn Apart by Unprecedented Numbers of Suicide Bombers

Robert Fisk

In the following viewpoint, Robert Fisk reports that an independent investigation estimates more than a thousand Muslim suicide bombers have blown themselves up in Iraq. Fisk analyzes the pattern of the attacks and notes that neither American nor Iraqi authorities have a clear idea who the bombers are or from where they come. Fisk is the Middle East correspondent for the Independent.

As you read, consider the following questions:

1. According to an investigation by the *Independent*, how many estimated Muslim suicide bombers have blown themselves up in Iraq between 2003 and 2008, as reported by the author?

2. How many Iraqi men, women, and children have been killed because of suicide bombers in Iraq during that period, according to the author?

3. According to Fisk, how many suicide attacks have been staged against Iraqi police or paramilitary forces?

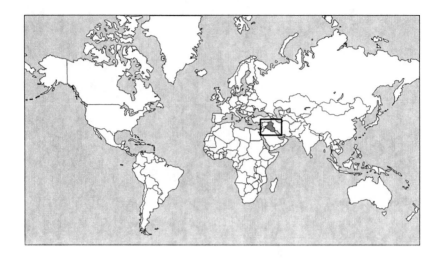

Khaled looked at me with a broad smile. He was almost laughing. At one point, when I told him that he should abandon all thoughts of being a suicide bomber—that he could influence more people in this world by becoming a journalist—he put his head back and shot me a grin, world-weary for a man in his teens. "You have your mission," he said. "And I have mine." His sisters looked at him in awe. He was their hero, their amanuensis and their teacher, their representative and their soon-to-be-martyred brother. Yes, he was handsome, young—just 18—he was dressed in a black Giorgio Armani T-shirt, a small, carefully trimmed Spanish conquistador's beard, gelled hair. And he was ready to immolate himself.

A sinister surprise. I had travelled to Khaled's home to speak to his mother. I had already written about his brother Hassan and wanted to introduce a Canadian journalist colleague, Nelofer Pazira, to the family. When Khaled walked on to the porch of the house, Nelofer and I both realised—at the same moment—that he was next, the next to die, the next "martyr". It was his smile. I've come across these young men before, but never one who so obviously declared his calling.

His family sat around us on the porch of their home above the Lebanese city of Sidon, the sitting room adorned with coloured photographs of Hassan, already gone to the paradise—so they assured me—for which Khaled clearly thought he was destined. Hassan had driven his explosives-laden car into an American military convoy at Tal Afar in northwestern Iraq, his body (or what was left of it) buried "in situ"—or so his mother was informed.

What is astonishing ... is the sheer scale of the suicide campaign, the vast numbers of young men (only occasionally women), who wilfully destroy themselves.

The Massive Scale of the Suicide Campaign

It's easy to find the families of the newly dead in Lebanon. Their names are read from the minarets of Sidon's mosques (most are Palestinian) and in Tripoli, in northern Lebanon, the Sunni "Tawhid" movement boasts "hundreds" of suiciders among its supporters. Every night, the population of Lebanon watches the brutal war in Iraq on television. "It's difficult to reach 'Palestine' these days," Khaled's uncle informed me. "Iraq is easier." Too true. No one doubts that the road to Baghdad—or Tal Afar or Fallujah or Mosul—lies through Syria, and that the movement of suicide bombers from the Mediterranean coasts to the deserts of Iraq is a planned if not particularly sophisticated affair. What is astonishing—what is not mentioned by the Americans or the Iraqi "government" or the British authorities or indeed by many journalists—is the sheer scale of the suicide campaign, the vast numbers of young men (only occasionally women), who wilfully destroy themselves amid the American convoys, outside the Iraqi police stations, in markets and around mosques and in shopping streets and on lonely roads beside remote checkpoints across the

179

huge cities and vast deserts of Iraq. Never have the true figures for this astonishing and unprecedented campaign of self-liquidation been calculated.

But a month-long investigation by the *Independent*, culling four Arabic-language newspapers, official Iraqi statistics, two Beirut news agencies and Western reports, shows that an incredible 1,121 Muslim suicide bombers have blown themselves up in Iraq. This is a very conservative figure and—given the propensity of the authorities (and of journalists) to report only those suicide bombings that kill dozens of people—the true estimate may be double this number. On several days, six—even nine—suicide bombers have exploded themselves in Iraq in a display of almost Wal-Mart availability. If life in Iraq is cheap, death is cheaper.

A Sickening Legacy

This is perhaps the most frightening and ghoulish legacy of George Bush's invasion of Iraq five years ago. Suicide bombers in Iraq have killed at least 13,000 men, women and children—our most conservative estimate gives a total figure of 13,132—and wounded a minimum of 16,112 people. If we include the dead and wounded in the mass stampede at the Baghdad Tigris River bridge in the summer of 2005—caused by fear of suicide bombers—the figures rise to 14,132 and 16,612 respectively. Again, it must be emphasised that these statistics are minimums. For 529 of the suicide bombings in Iraq, no figures for wounded are available. Where wounded have been listed in news reports as "several", we have made no addition to the figures. And the number of critically injured who later died remains unknown. Set against a possible death toll of half a million Iraqis since the March 2003 invasion, the suicide bombers' victims may appear insignificant; but the killers' ability to terrorise civilians, militiamen and Western troops and mercenaries is incalculable.

Never before has the Arab world witnessed a phenomenon of suicide-death on this scale. During Israel's occupation of Lebanon after 1982, one Hizbollah suicide-bombing a month was considered remarkable. During the Palestinian intifadas [uprisings] of the 1980s and 1990s, four per month was regarded as unprecedented. But suicide bombers in Iraq have been attacking at the average rate of two every three days since the 2003 Anglo-American invasion.

The killers' ability to terrorise civilians, militiamen and Western troops and mercenaries is incalculable.

The Identity of the Perpetrators

And, although neither the Iraqi government nor their American mentors will admit this, scarcely 10 out of more than a thousand suicide killers have been identified. We know from their families that Palestinians, Saudis, Syrians and Algerians have been among the bombers. In a few cases, we have names. But in most attacks, the authorities in Iraq—if they can still be called "authorities" after five years of catastrophe—have no idea to whom the bloodied limbs and headless torsos of the bombers belong. Even more profoundly disturbing is that the "cult" of the suicide bomber has seeped across national frontiers. Within a year of the Iraqi invasion, Afghan Taliban bombers were blowing themselves up alongside Western troops or bases in Helmand province and in the capital, Kabul. The practice leached into Pakistan, striking down thousands of troops and civilians, killing even the principal opposition leader, Benazir Bhutto. The London Tube and bus bombings—despite the denials of [British Prime Minister] Tony Blair—were obviously deeply influenced by events in Iraq.

Academics and politicians have long debated the motives of the bombers, the psychological makeup of the men and women who cold-bloodedly decide to undertake the role of suicide executioners; for they are executioners, killers who see their victims—be they soldiers or civilians—before they flick the switch that destroys them. The Israelis long ago decided that there was no "perfect" profile for a suicide bomber, and my own experience in Lebanon bears this out. The suicider might have spent years fighting the Israelis in the south of the country. Often, they would have been imprisoned or tortured by Israel or its proxy Lebanese militia. Sometimes, brothers or other family members would have been killed. On other occasions, the example of their own relatives would have drawn them into the vortex of suicide-by-example.

Suicide Bombers vs. Kamikazes

Khaled is—or was, for I no longer know if he is alive, since I met him a few weeks ago—influenced by his brother Hassan, whose journey to Iraq was organised by an unknown group, presumably Palestinian, and whose weapons training beside the Tigris River was videotaped by his comrades. Hassan's mother has shown me this tape—which ends with Hassan cheerfully waving goodbye from the driver's window of a battered car, presumably the vehicle he was about to ram into the American convoy at Tal Afar. None of this addresses the issue of religious belief. While there is evidence aplenty that the Japanese suicide pilots of the Second World War were sometimes coerced and intimidated into their final flights against US warships in the Pacific, many also believed that they were dying for their emperor. For them, the fall of cherry blossom and the divine wind—the "kamikaze"—blessed their souls as they aimed their bombers at American aircraft carriers. But even an industrialised dictatorship like Japan—facing the imminent collapse of its entire society at the hands of a superpower—could only mobilise 4,615 "kamikazes". The Iraq suicide bombers may already have reached half that number.

But the Japanese authorities encouraged their pilots to think of themselves as a collective suicide unit whose insignia of imminent death—white Rising Sun headbands and white scarves—prefigured the yellow headbands imprinted with Koranic script that Hizbollah guerrillas wore when they set out to attack Israeli soldiers in the occupied zone of southern Lebanon. In Iraq, however, those who direct the growing army of suiciders do not lack inventiveness. Their bombers have arrived at the scene of their self-destruction dressed as car mechanics, soldiers, police officers, middle-aged housewives, children's sweet sellers, worshippers and—on one occasion—a "harmless" shepherd. They have carried their bombs in Oldsmobiles, fuel trucks, garbage trucks, flatbed trucks, on donkeys and bicycles, motor bikes and mopeds and carts, minibuses, date-vendors' vans, mobile recruitment centres and lorries packed with chlorine. Incredibly, there appears to be no individual central "brain" behind the bombings—although "groupuscules" of bombers obviously exist. Inspiration, imitation and the globalised influence of the Internet appear sufficient to empower the bombers of Iraq.

Families Are Supportive of Bombers

On an individual level, it is possible to see the friction and psychological trauma of families. Khaled's mother, for instance, constantly expressed her pride in her dead son Hassan and, in front of me, she looked with almost equal love at his still-living brother. But when my companion urged Khaled to remain alive for his mother's sake—reminding him that the Prophet himself spoke of the primary obligation of a Muslim man to protect his mother—the woman was close to tears. She was torn apart by her love as a mother and her religious-political duty as the woman who had brought another would-be martyr into the world. When my friend again urged Khaled to remain alive, to stay in Sidon and marry—eerily, the muezzin's call to prayer had begun during our conversation—he shook his head.

Not even a disparaging remark about those who would send him on his death mission—that they were prepared to live in this world while sending others like Khaled to their fate—could discourage him. "I am not going to become a 'shahed' [martyr] for people," he replied. "I am doing it for God."

It was the same old argument. We could produce a hundred good ways—peaceful ways—for him to resolve the injustices of this world; but the moment Khaled invoked the name of God, our suggestions became irrelevant. Rationality—humanism, if you like—simply withered away. If a Western president could invoke a war of "good against evil", his antagonists could do the same.

Discerning a Pattern

But is there a rational pattern to the suicide bombings in Iraq? The first incidents of their kind took place as American troops were actually advancing towards Baghdad. Near the Shia town of Nasiriyah, an off-duty Iraqi policeman, Sergeant Ali Jaffar Moussa Hamadi al-Nomani, drove a car bomb into an American Marine roadblock. Married, with five children, he had been a soldier in Iraq's 1980–88 war with Iran and had volunteered to fight the Americans after Saddam's [referring to former president of Iraq Saddam Hussein] occupation of Kuwait. Shortly afterwards, two Shia Muslim women did the same.

In its dying days, even Saddam Hussein's own government was shocked. "The US administration is going to turn the whole world into people prepared to die for their nations," Saddam's vice-president, Taha Yassin Ramadan, warned. "All they can do now is turn themselves into bombs. If the B-52 bombs can now kill 500 or more in our war, then I'm sure that some operations by our freedom fighters will be able to kill 5,000." Ramadan even referred to "the martyr's moment of sublimity"—an al-Qa'ida-like phrase that ill befitted a secular Baathist—and it was clear that the vice-president was almost as surprised as the Americans. But only two days after the US occupation of Baghdad, a woman killed herself while trying to explode a grenade among a group of American troops outside the capital.

The Main Targets

Throughout the five years of war, suicide bombers have focused on Iraq's own American-trained security forces rather than US troops. At least 365 attacks have been staged against Iraqi police or paramilitary forces. Their targets included at least 147 police stations (1,577 deaths), 43 army and police recruitment centres (939 deaths), 91 checkpoints (with a minimum of 564 fatalities), 92 security patrols (465 deaths) and numerous other police targets (escorts, convoys accompanying government ministers, etc.). One of the recruitment centres—in the centre of Baghdad—was assaulted by suicide bombers on eight separate occasions.

By contrast, suicide bombers have attacked only 24 US bases at a cost of 100 American dead and 15 Iraqis, and 43 American patrols and checkpoints, during which 116 US personnel were killed along with at least 56 civilians, 15 of whom appear to have been shot by American soldiers in response to the attacks, and another 26 of whom were children standing next to a US patrol. Most of the Americans were killed west or north of Baghdad. Suicide attacks on the police concentrated on Baghdad and Mosul and the Sunni towns to the immediate north and south of Baghdad.

The trajectory of the suicide bombers shows a clear preference for military targets throughout the insurgency, with attacks on Americans gradually decreasing from 2006 and individual attacks on Iraqi police patrols and police recruits increasing over the past two years, especially in the 100 miles north of Baghdad. Just as the Islamist murderers of Algeria—and their military opponents—favoured the fasting month of Ramadan for their bloodiest assaults in the 1990s, so the suicide bombers of Iraq mobilise on the eve of religious festivals.

There was a pronounced drop in suicide assaults during the period of sectarian liquidations after 2005, either because the bombers feared interception by the throat-cutters of tribal gangs working their way across Baghdad, or because—a grim possibility—they were themselves being used in the sectarian murder campaign.

Attacks That Have the Most Impact

The most politically powerful attacks occurred inside military bases—including the Green Zone in Baghdad (two in one day in October 2004)—and against the UN [United Nations] headquarters (in which the UN envoy Sergio de Mello was killed) and the International Red Cross offices in Baghdad in 2003. By December 2003, British officials were warning that there were more "spectacular" suicide bombings to come, and the first suicide assault on a mosque took place in January of the following year when a bomber on a bicycle blew himself up in a Shia mosque in Baquba, killing four worshippers and wounding another 39.

Scarcely a year later, another suicider attacked a second Shia mosque, killing 14 worshippers and wounding 40. In February 2004, a man blew himself up on a bus outside the Shia mosque at Khadamiyah in Baghdad, killing 17 more Shia Muslims. Only a few days earlier, a man wearing an explosives belt killed four at yet another Shia mosque in the Doura district of Baghdad. The suicide campaign against Shia places of worship continued with an attack on a Mosul mosque in March 2005, killing at least 50, two more attacks in April that killed 26, and another in May in Baghdad.

While Shia mosques were being targeted in a deliberate campaign of provocation by al-Qa'ida-type suiciders, markets and hospitals frequented by Shia Muslims were also attacked. Almost all the 600 Iraqis killed by suicide bombs in May 2005 were Shias. After the partial demolition of the Shia mosque at Samarra on 22 February 2006, the "war of the mosques" began in earnest for the suicide bombers of Iraq. A Sunni mosque was blown up, with nine dead and "dozens" of wounded, and two Shia mosques were the target of suicide bombers in the same week. In early July 2006, seven suicide killers blew themselves up in Sunni and Shia mosques, leaving a total of 51 civilians dead. During the same period, a suicide bomber launched the first attack of its kind on Shia pilgrims arriving from Iran.

Bombers were to attack the funerals of those Shia they had killed, and even wedding parties. Schools, university campuses and shopping precincts were also now included on the target lists, most of the victims yet again being Shia. Over the past year, however, an increasing number of tribal leaders loyal to the Americans—including Sattar Abu Risha, who publicly met President [George W.] Bush on 13 September 2007, and former insurgents who have now joined the American-paid anti-al-Qa'ida militias—have been blown apart by Sunni bombers.

Little Intelligence on the Killers

Only about 10 of the suicide bombers have been identified. One of them, who attacked an Iraqi police unit in June 2005, turned out to be a former police commando called Abu Mohamed al-Dulaimi, but the Americans and the Iraqi authorities appear to have little intelligence on the provenance of these killers. On at least 27 occasions, Iraqi officials have claimed to know the identity of the killers—saying that they had recovered passports and identity papers that proved their "foreign" origin—but they have never produced these documents for public inspection. There is even doubt that the two suicide bombers who blew themselves up in a bird market earlier this year were in fact mentally retarded young women, as the government was to allege.

Indeed, nothing could better illustrate the lack of knowledge of the authorities than the two contradictory statements made by the Americans and their Iraqi protégés in March of last year. Just as David Satterfield, US Secretary of State Condoleezza Rice's adviser on Iraq, was claiming that "90 per cent" of suicide bombers were crossing the border from Syria, Iraq's Prime Minister, Nuri al-Maliki, was announcing that "most" of the suiciders came from Saudi Arabia—which shares a long, common border with Iraq. Saudis would hardly waste their time travelling to Damascus to cross a border that their own country shared with Iraq. Many in Baghdad, including some government ministers, believe that the nationality of the bombers is much closer to home—that they are, in fact, Iraqis.

One of George Bush's most insidious legacies in Iraq thus remains its most mysterious—the marriage of nationalism and spiritual ferocity, the birth of an unprecedentedly huge army of Muslims inspired by the idea of death.

US Needs a Clearer Idea of the Problem

It will be many years before we have a clearer idea of the number of bombers who have killed themselves in the Iraq war—and of their origin. Long before the *Independent*'s total figure reached 500, al-Qa'ida's Abu Musab al-Zarqawi was boasting of "800 martyrs" among his supporters. And since al-Zarqawi's death brought not the slightest reduction in bombings, we must assume that there are many other "manipulators" in charge of Iraq's suicide squads.

Nor can we assume the motives for every mass murder. Who now remembers that the greatest individual number of victims of any suicide bombing died in two remote villages of the Kahtaniya region of Iraq, all Yazidis—516 of them slaughtered, another 525 wounded. A Yazidi girl, it seems, had fallen in love with a Sunni man and had been punished by her own people for this "honour crime": She had been stoned to death. The killers presumably came from the Sunni community.

One of George Bush's most insidious legacies in Iraq thus remains its most mysterious—the marriage of nationalism and spiritual ferocity, the birth of an unprecedentedly huge army of Muslims inspired by the idea of death.

Al Qaeda Recruits Female Suicide Bombers in Iraq

Kholoud Ramzi

In the following viewpoint, Kholoud Ramzi investigates the trend of female suicide bombers in Iraq, reporting that these women are recruited by al Qaeda and are often pressured or forced into their final roles. She observes that Iraqi security forces have organized a special women's terrorist task force in hopes that it will reverse the trend and decrease the number of suicide bombings in the country. Ramzi is a contributor to Niqash, a website for Iraqi debate and views.

As you read, consider the following questions:

1. How many female suicide bombings were perpetrated in Iraq from January–August 2008, as reported by the author?

2. According to Ramzi, how many female suicide bombings were carried out in Iraq from 2006–2008?

3. According to the author, what is the "Daughters of Diyala"?

Sumaya will never forget the day when armed al-Qaeda men forced her to practice wearing an explosive vest under her clothes in preparation for a suicide attack on a local market she was supposed to carry out the following day.

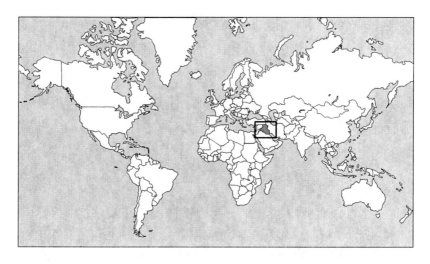

Sumaya's story began when her husband, Amjad al-Dulaimi, a former officer in the Iraqi army, joined al-Qaeda's ranks after being recruited by former army colleagues. He had refused when first approached because he feared that his family would be targeted. But, "under financial pressure and with a lack of work opportunities" he was forced to join al-Qaeda, says his wife.

Amjad undertook many tasks such as planting explosive devices on roads, transporting small rockets, attacking army and police convoys and other similar tasks making use of his previous military experience. After less than one year, Amjad was surprised when al-Qaeda's emir, responsible for his group, ordered the recruitment of women jihadis. Amjad and four other men in his group brought their wives thinking that they would be required to perform "easy tasks" such as gathering information for fighters.

A Forced Recruitment

The next day, the emir arrived with a woman he introduced as a "sister in jihad." Without revealing her real name, the woman met with the five wives and after a half-an-hour meeting she emerged to tell the emir that she has chosen Amjad's wife to implement a suicide attack.

Al-Qaeda offered Amjad $5000 in compensation to help him raise his three children. "I still recall those moments when the emir started thanking God and congratulating me for the choice of my wife to become the martyr. I recalled the years I spent in the army away from my family and the hardships Sumaya suffered providing for the family needs. I recalled all these memories while the emir was telling me to recite the Quran as many times as possible and to prepare my wife for the attack."

"This was a crucial test after which I decided to walk away," says Amjad. It only took him a few hours to decide to leave al-Ghazaliyah, northwest of Baghdad, where he had lived for more than 20 years and to escape that same day with his wife and family, leaving behind all his possessions, only fearing the consequences if they failed to reach a safe haven before his escape was discovered. The family headed to the Shiite Sadr City, a location beyond the reach of his former al-Qaeda comrades, and lived there with the help of old friends.

The process of recruiting female bombers began when Sajida al-Rishawi was recruited for a joint attack with her husband on a Jordanian hotel in 2005.

According to Sumaya, the request to participate in an attack came totally out of the blue. "When the emir asked my husband to bring me with him, I thought that these people wanted to benefit from the nature of my work as a teacher in order to collect information on the area and its people but I was surprised to be the one chosen for the attack."

Sumaya said that the "sister in jihad" told them that al-Qaeda wanted to quickly prepare for an attack. "I am obliged to choose the one who is most capable of hiding her load of ammunition." After a test, she praised the way Sumaya walked carrying a heavy vest of stones and chose her for the task.

Fear prompted Sumaya to cry out. "But I am a mother of three children!" she exclaimed. It was then that the lady told her: "Do not worry about them, we will guarantee their future."

A Disturbing Trend

Sumaya is only one among many female suicide bombers al-Qaeda has attempted to recruit to carry out attacks in Iraq, but one of the very few fortunate enough to escape. The process of recruiting female bombers began when Sajida al-Rishawi was recruited for a joint attack with her husband on a Jordanian hotel in 2005.

According to statistics from the Ministry of Interior, 356 people were killed and injured in 16 suicide attacks carried out by women since the beginning of 2008. Another 34 attacks were carried out by al-Qaeda women during the last two years. According to information made available to Niqash, the majority of female suicide bombers are trained at a special female camp established by al-Qaeda in Diyala province.

Countering the Trend

In response, security and tribal authorities in Diyala have recently created a special women's force specifically to combat female violence. Composed of 150 women trained by US forces, the unit, named the "Daughters of Diyala", is similar to the armies of awakening councils. It aims to prevent further suicide attacks by al-Qaeda women in security turbulent Diyala province. Awakening councils in Baghdad also initiated a similar endeavor when 100 women volunteered to be trained by US female soldiers on detecting and combating female suicide bombers.

Government officials hope that these endeavors will contribute towards reducing the number of suicide attacks carried out by women. Adnan al-Asadi, undersecretary for the Iraqi interior minister, told Niqash that "security forces have re-

"Suicide Bomber," cartoon by Kjell Nilsson-Maki, www.CartoonStock.com. Copyright © by Kjell Nilsson-Maki. Reproduction rights obtainable from www.CartoonStock.com.

corded 79 attacks by women suicide bombers since the US entry into Iraq in April 2003." He said that as emirs and leaders of armed cells have had to go into hiding following recent government security operations, more women have been recruited for attacks.

"The last two months have witnessed seven suicide bombings by women; three were carried out in one day targeting a group of Shiite visitors to the al-Karadah area in Baghdad and the latest was an attack by a 15-year-old girl. An investigation confirmed that the girl was intoxicated when she carried out the attack," he said.

Security and tribal authorities in Diyala have recently created a special women's force specifically to combat female violence.

Poverty and Female Suicide Bombers

According to al-Asadi "al-Qaeda has succeeded in mobilizing women suffering from poverty and ignorance as well as widowed women to become suicide bombers. In some cases, belts containing explosive materials have been given to women in order to be delivered to certain people in return for a large sum of money. The explosives carried by these women were then detonated using a remote control device. Sometimes, street girls, not yet 18 years old, have been recruited."

Yasin al-Azzawi, a social researcher, attributes the reason for women recruits to "the free mobility of women who do not undergo inspection by police and army checkpoints. Thus it is easier for them to carry out such attacks."

Based on his research over the last two years, al-Azzawi notes that "there has been a big increase in the number of women joining terrorist groups following the relative success of awakening councils in defeating al-Qaeda." He points out that "Islamist hard-liners banned women from participating in jihad against the West before they changed their strategy. In al-Qaeda and Taliban military camps in Afghanistan, women were separated from their husbands and were asked to care for their children to allow men to dedicate their lives to jihad, but in Iraq a need for women's participation was created when men's activities became easily detected and hence women became an important factor in Islamic terrorism," he said.

South Russia Is Threatened by Suicide Car Bombings and Sectarian Violence

Kyiv Post

The Kyiv Post *is the Ukraine's leading English-language newspaper. In the following viewpoint, the reporter covers a tragic suicide car bombing outside of a crowded market in the Republic of North Ossetia-Alania that killed seventeen people and injured many more. The paper reveals that the attack was blamed on Islamic militants trying to incite a wider conflict between ethnic Ossetians, who are predominantly Orthodox Christian, and ethnic Ingush, who are predominantly Sufi Muslim.*

As you read, consider the following questions:

1. How many times had the market been bombed in the past decade, as reported by the author?
2. According to the author, when did open fighting between Ossetians and Ingush begin in the region?
3. How many people were killed in the Beslan siege in 2004, according to the author?

Russian Prime Minister Vladimir Putin blamed extremists "without souls, without hearts" for a suicide car bombing that killed 17 people in the crowded central market of a city in the North Caucasus.

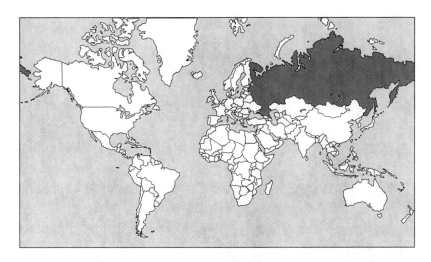

It was the fourth terrorist attack at the market in a decade, and while no one claimed responsibility, the Kremlin has been trying to contain Islamic militancy in the mountainous southern region of Russia.

Nearly 140 were wounded in the bombing Thursday in Vladikavkaz, the capital of North Ossetia, with about a half dozen hospitalized in very serious condition.

Putin met with Russia's top Muslim cleric after the blast and said Russia's estimated 20 million Muslims should play a key role in eradicating Islamic extremism in the nation.

"The crimes like the one that was committed in the North Caucasus today are aimed at sowing enmity between our citizens. We mustn't allow this," Putin said in televised remarks at the meeting.

The bomber drove to the market's main entrance and detonated the explosives, the Emergency Situations Ministry said. The blast tore the car in half, littered the market square with shrapnel and blew out windows in nearby buildings, according to nationally broadcast video that also showed charred body parts—presumably those of the bomber—bloodstains on the pavement and rows of scarred vehicles.

"The Psychology of Terror," cartoon by Wilfred Hildonen, www.CartoonStock.com. Copyright © by Wilfred Hildonen. Reproduction rights obtainable from www.Cartoon Stock.com.

The bomber was identified as a resident of neighboring Ingushetia, the independent Kavkazsky Uzel website reported, quoting an unidentified official.

The death toll included the bomber, and 98 of the 138 people wounded in the explosion were hospitalized, said Alexander Pogorely of the Emergency Situations Ministry. The RIA Novosti news agency said six ethnic Ingush were among the wounded.

Three suspected accomplices of the bomber were detained, federal security chief Alexander Bortnikov said in televised remarks.

Putin blamed the violence on "people without souls, without hearts. They literally hold nothing sacred. Our common duty is to fight these crimes, these criminals."

The attack came as Muslims prepared for the feast that celebrates the end of the holy month of Ramadan.

Unlike the provinces of Chechnya, Ingushetia and Dagestan, where Muslims make up most of the population, North Ossetia is predominantly Orthodox Christian. It has been destabilized by long-simmering tensions between ethnic Ossetians and ethnic Ingush that exploded into an open fighting in 1992.

President Barack Obama condemned the attack and said it underscores the resolution of Washington and Moscow to cooperate in fighting terrorism.

"Our hearts go out to the people of North Ossetia, who have already suffered so much from horrific acts of terrorism," he said in a statement.

Russian President Dmitry Medvedev immediately sent his regional envoy to Vladikavkaz to help coordinate efforts to help the victims. He urged investigators to "do everything to track down the freaks, the lowlifes who conducted that terror attack."

The regional president of Ingushetia, Yunus-Bek Yevkurov, quickly sent condolences to the leader of North Ossetia to help assuage tensions between the two ethnic groups.

Russia's ethnically diverse North Caucasus region has been gripped by violence stemming from two separatist wars in Chechnya and fueled by endemic poverty and rampant official corruption.

It was the deadliest attack in the region since a double suicide bombing killed 12 in nearby Dagestan in April. Twin suicide bombings on Moscow subway in March killed 40 people and wounded over 100.

Russia's ethnically diverse North Caucasus region has been gripped by violence stemming from two separatist wars in Chechnya and fueled by endemic poverty and rampant official corruption. Human rights groups say law enforcement officers frequently resort to extrajudicial killings, kidnappings and torture, breeding hostility and provoking retaliatory attacks.

The Vladikavkaz market area has been the target of several bomb attacks in the past dozen years in which scores of people have died. A 1999 bombing killed 55 people. Another explosion in 2001 killed six, and in 2004, 11 people died when a minibus near the market was bombed.

North Ossetia was also the scene of the 2004 Beslan siege, where Chechen militants took hundreds of hostages at a school. It ended in a bloodbath in which more than 330 people, about half of them children, were killed.

China's Xinjiang Region Is Rocked by Female Suicide Bombers

Richard Lloyd Parry

Richard Lloyd Parry is a reporter for the Times. *In the following viewpoint, he describes a coordinated attack by separatist insurgents in the Xinjiang region of China, the homeland of the Uighur people. Parry reports that two of the attackers were female—the first case of female suicide bombers being used in such terrorist attacks in China.*

As you read, consider the following questions:

1. How many people were killed in the coordinated attacks, as reported by the author?
2. According to Parry, how many of the bombers survived?
3. How many separate attacks were there, according to the author?

Two women, including a teenage girl, were among the suicide attackers who launched a series of bomb attacks on a police station, government offices and shops, according to a senior official in China's troubled northwestern region of Xinjiang.

Chinese police in black body armour and carrying machine guns and rifles hunted for three escaped suspects yester-

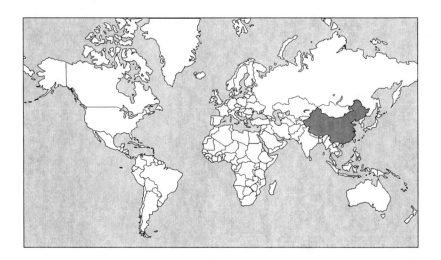

day [in August 2008], after the attacks on Sunday morning, the latest in a series of violent incidents apparently carried out by separatist insurgents and timed to coincide with the Beijing Olympics.

The Female Killers

A 15-year-old girl identified as Hailiqiemu Abulizi was said to be in a stable condition last night, after being injured when a homemade bomb exploded prematurely. She underwent surgery after suffering 17 separate injuries, including a broken leg and foot.

Another woman, who has not been identified by the authorities, died after setting off a bomb which she was carrying in order to avoid imminent capture as she and four of her fellow attackers were cornered in a bazaar in the oasis town of Kuqa in China's Xinjiang region. According to the Chinese authorities, ten of the attackers died in the attack, all of them Uighurs, a Muslim people who form the biggest ethnic group in Xinjiang.

A Uighur passerby who was caught up in the attacks died in hospital yesterday, the second man to be killed by the bombings which injured five others. Three of the attackers were arrested, and ten died, including two who killed themselves with their own bombs.

"If they are [Uighur] nationalists, then why didn't they attack Chinese people?" asked Mu Tielifuhasimu, head of Aksu prefecture of which Kuqa is part. "They actually killed two Uighur people, and injured other innocent people in the streets."

In fact, the seventeen separate attacks seem to have been planned with the intention of avoiding harm to Uighurs or civilians.

The Plan

In fact the seventeen separate attacks seem to have been planned with the intention of avoiding harm to Uighurs or civilians. They began at about 2:30 in the morning, a time when few people were on the streets, and were directed at the police headquarters, a government building and shops and businesses owned by ethnic Han Chinese, whom some Uighurs resent as colonialist interlopers.

A Chaotic Scene

Witnesses, most of whom refused to give their names, described chaotic early morning scenes as armed police hunted down the fleeing attackers through the back alleys of Kuqa. The bloody end came at around 8:30 a.m. with a last desperate stand among the empty stalls and shops of the night bazaar. A two-minute film shot by one man on his camera phone from a high building overlooking the scene, and obtained by the *Times*, shows police cars driving down the street, and figures running for cover, while a voice, presumably that of a policeman, barks through a megaphone.

"I live nearby and I could hear explosions and shooting," a Chinese man named Ma said. "Judging from the noise, there were a lot of explosions. I peeped out and saw police everywhere, coming from every direction to arrest them." Most traces of the attacks had been cleared up by yesterday, although there were still fragments of broken glass in front of a row of damaged shops and windows close to the market that were pierced by bullet holes.

A Terrorist Attack

Mr Mu said that the attackers were all Uighurs, but said that it was too early to draw conclusions about their motives or whether they were members of an organisation. He also declined to speculate on a link with an attack eight days ago in which 16 police were killed in the Xinjiang city of Kashgar by two men who drove a lorry into them, stabbed and bombed them.

But there are no plausible candidates other than the shadowy groups who, over the years, have called for independence for the region which they refer to as East Turkestan. "I think we are seeing an upturn in Uighur militancy," said Nicholas Bequelin, a researcher based in Hong Kong for Human Rights Watch, and an expert on Xinjiang.

"This [series of attacks on Monday] is unprecedented in terms of its organisation. It is an incredible act of defiance during the Olympics, a moment most precious to the government when they most want to avoid any kind of trouble or separatist violence." He said that the use of female suicide attackers appeared to be a first.

Journalists working in Kuqa were closely monitored by police and officials and the *Times* photographer, Jack Hill, was detained for hours yesterday after Kuqa police insisted that the identity documents issued by Beijing police were inadequate. He was eventually released after intervention from Mr Mu, but forbidden from taking photographs in the town.

Periodical and Internet Sources Bibliography

The following articles have been selected to supplement the diverse views presented in this chapter.

Marc Bastian	"Teenage Fighters on Frontline of Afghan War," *China Daily*, February 9, 2011.
Chosun Ilbo	"'Human Torpedoes' Are the North's Secret Naval Weapon," April 22, 2010.
Vikram Dodd	"The Drink Bottle That Could Have Downed a Plane," *Guardian*, September 7, 2009.
Gwynne Dyer	"Not Enough Latex Gloves?" *Zimbabwe Independent*, January 14, 2010.
Miriam Elder	"Should Airports Secure Arrivals Halls?" GlobalPost, January 28, 2011. www.globalpost.com.
Paul Kix	"The Truth About Suicide Bombers," *Boston Globe*, December 5, 2010.
Ben Knight	"Caucasus Is Threatening to Become Russia's Iraq," Deutsche Welle, January 25, 2011. www.dw-world.de.
Stuart Littlewood	"Will Israel Spark New Wave of Suicide Bomber?" *Palestine Chronicle*, March 8, 2010.
Ali Mohammed	"Would-Be Suicide Bomber Recalls Failed Mission," Institute for War & Peace Reporting, August 5, 2010. http://iwpr.net.
Sharmeen Obaid-Chinoy	"Children Taught to Be Suicide Bombers," CNN.com, June 15, 2010. www.cnn.com.
Marcus Oscarsson	"Suicide Bombing Shocks Sweden," GlobalPost, December 12, 2010. www.globalpost.com.
Richard Spencer	"A History of Hezbollah," *Daily Telegraph*, January 12, 2011.

For Further Discussion

Chapter 1

1. What factors influence suicide rates in different countries and regions? Which do you feel are key to lowering the suicide rate and why?

2. In several countries discussed in this book, there are no accurate statistics on how many people commit suicide. How does a lack of reliable statistics hinder a full understanding of the scope of the suicide problem in some countries?

Chapter 2

1. A number of countries are discussing or implementing assisted suicide policies. In this chapter, you read about how England is approaching the issue. What is your opinion on the issue? How do you think it should be treated in your country?

2. The viewpoints in this chapter examine various suicide prevention policies and strategies. Which one do you feel will be successful? Do any stand out as insufficient in light of the problem?

Chapter 3

1. A few of the viewpoints in this chapter discuss the rise of suicides in the workplace. What factors in the workplace do you think contribute to suicide attempts? How can businesses address this problem?

2. It is clear from the viewpoints in this chapter that political circumstances may contribute to suicide rates. Point to an example in the book. How can the government develop policies or strategies to impact suicide trends?

Chapter 4

1. What is the role of women in the practice of suicide bombing? How are women forced to become suicide bombers?

2. From reading the viewpoints in this chapter, what factors motivate suicide bombers? How can governments craft policies to address this problem?

Organizations to Contact

The editors have compiled the following list of organizations concerned with the issues debated in this book. The descriptions are derived from materials provided by the organizations. All have publications or information available for interested readers. The list was compiled on the date of publication of the present volume; the information provided here may change. Be aware that many organizations take several weeks or longer to respond to inquiries, so allow as much time as possible.

American Foundation for Suicide Prevention (AFSP)

120 Wall Street, 22nd Floor, New York, NY   10005
(888) 333-2377 • fax: (212) 363-6237
e-mail: inquiry@afsp.org
website: www.afsp.org

The American Foundation for Suicide Prevention (AFSP) is a national nonprofit organization that aims to decrease suicide rates through research, education, and advocacy for sound mental health policies. AFSP is determined to reach out to those considering suicide as well as those affected by the tragedy of suicide. Many of the organization's programs are geared toward survivors of suicide and people at risk. The AFSP publishes a quarterly newsletter, *Lifesavers*, which explores the foundation's recent initiatives and events as well as mental health and suicide prevention topics. The AFSP website provides access to *Lifesavers*; educational material; information on chapters, recent awareness campaigns, and upcoming events; important research; press releases; and breaking news.

Canadian Association for Suicide Prevention (CASP)

870 Portage Avenue, Winnipeg, MB   R3G 0P1
   Canada
(204) 784-4073
e-mail: casp@casp-acps.ca
website: www.suicideprevention.ca

The Canadian Association for Suicide Prevention (CASP) is a national nonprofit organization formed to disseminate suicide prevention information to all Canadians. It also advocates for effective mental health policies and provides support for those affected by the specter of suicide. CASP and other mental health groups developed the Blueprint for Canadian National Suicide Prevention Strategy, a national suicide prevention plan. The organization publishes a newsletter, *CASP News*, which is available on the CASP website. Also featured on the website is a calendar of upcoming events; the latest news and updates about key campaigns, research and statistics about suicide in Canada; and guidelines and fact sheets.

Centers for Disease Control and Prevention (CDC)
1600 Clifton Road, Atlanta, GA   30333
(800) CDC-INFO
e-mail: cdcinfo@cdc.gov
website: www.cdc.gov

The Centers for Disease Control and Prevention (CDC), a federal agency that operates as part of the Department of Health and Human Services, was established to protect public health and safety. The CDC has developed a National Strategy for Suicide Prevention through one of its agencies, the Substance Abuse and Mental Health Services Administration (SAMHSA). The CDC website offers a range of national statistics, fact sheets, research, and suicide prevention information in text and podcast. It also features access to *Preventing Suicide: Program Activities Guide*, which describes the CDC's suicide prevention activities.

Citizens United Resisting Euthanasia (CURE)
303 Truman Street, Berkeley Springs, WV   25411
(304) 258-LIFE
e-mail: cureltd@verizon.net
website: http://myplace.frontier.com/~vze7zk68

Citizens United Resisting Euthanasia (CURE) was founded in 1981 to oppose the practice of euthanasia. Consisting of patient advocates, religious figures, health care professionals, and activists, CURE lobbies against legislation that supports the legalization of assisted suicide. One of the organization's key activities is education; to this end, it makes available materials and essays to disseminate information on right-to-life issues and suicide prevention and offers rebuttals to pro-euthanasia talking points. The CURE website also links to the latest news and updates on recent anti-euthanasia efforts.

Compassion & Choices
PO Box 101810, Denver, CO   80250
(800) 247-7421 • fax: (866) 312-2690
website: www.compassionandchoices.org

Compassion & Choices is a nonprofit organization that aims to improve end-of-life care and provide choices for patients facing death decisions. The organization also offers support programs, including counseling and consultation with professional staff and trained volunteers; education through media outreach and print and online materials; and advocacy for legal and legislative initiatives that support a range of end-of-life options for those seeking them. The Compassion & Choices website provides access to press releases, promotional material, information on recent legal cases, fact sheets, and a catalog of books available through the organization.

International Association for Suicide Prevention (IASP)
National Centre for Suicide Research and Prevention
Sognsvannsveien 21, Bygg 12, Oslo   N-0372
   Norway
(+47) 229 237 15 • fax: (+47) 229 239 15
website: www.iasp.org

The International Association for Suicide Prevention (IASP) is an international organization "dedicated to preventing suicidal behavior; to alleviating its effects; to providing a forum for academicians, mental health professionals, crisis workers, volunteers, and suicide survivors." One of IASP's key aims is to raise suicide awareness around the world. IASP publishes *NewsBulletin*, an e-newsletter that explores global suicide prevention efforts and updates recent campaigns and events. The organization also publishes the *Journal of Crisis Intervention and Suicide Prevention*, which offers the latest research and analysis of suicide trends.

Mental Health America (MHA)

2000 North Beauregard Street, 6th Floor
Alexandria, VA   22311
(703) 684-7722 • fax: (703) 684-5968
e-mail: infoctr@mentalhealthamerica.net
website: www.nmha.org

Mental Health America (MHA) is a national advocacy organization that serves individuals with mental health and substance abuse issues. MHA educates and advocates for effective and fair mental health programs and policies, including suicide outreach and prevention. The MHA website features the latest news, fact sheets on key issues, educational materials, position briefs, a blog, and updates on recent events. MHA also publishes *The Bell*, which offers information on the organization's recent efforts.

Organisation for Economic Co-operation and Development (OECD)

2 Rue Andre Pascal, Paris Cedex 16   75775
   France
(+33) 1 45 24 82 00 • fax: (+33) 1 45 24 85 00
website: www.oecd.org

The Organisation for Economic Co-operation and Development (OECD) was established in 1961 to promote beneficial economic and social policies and to measure productivity and global trade. Because suicide is a trend that can endanger social well-being and economic productivity, the OECD compiles statistics on suicide rates and the efficacy of government intervention and suicide prevention policies. The organization also compares and analyzes suicide trends and statistics. The statistics and analyses can be found on the OECD website.

Suicide Prevention International (SPI)
1045 Park Avenue, Suite 3C, New York, NY   10028
website: www.spiorg.org

Suicide Prevention International (SPI) is an international nonprofit organization that develops, implements, and funds suicide prevention programs all over the world. A few of the organization's major projects include developing a mental health service network in rural China and suicide prevention programs in Vietnam. SPI publishes a series of research papers examining global suicide trends and the progress of SPI programs and policies. The SPI website also provides updates on the organization's events and research projects.

World Federation of Right to Die Societies (WF)
e-mail: wfsecretary@hotmail.com
website: www.worldrtd.net

The World Federation of Right to Die Societies is made up of thirty-three right-to-die associations from twenty-five countries. According to the federation, the organization's mission is to provide "an international link for organizations working to secure or protect the rights of individuals to self-determination at the end of their lives." The WF publishes a monthly online newsletter that collects right-to-die news from all over the world. Current news and updates on WF programs can be found on the organization's website.

World Health Organization (WHO)
Avenue Appia 20, Geneva 27   1211
   Switzerland
(+41) 22 791 21 11 • fax: (+41) 22 791 31 11
e-mail: info@who.int
website: www.who.int

The World Health Organization (WHO) is the United Nations agency tasked with directing and coordinating health research, analyses, and action. It provides global leadership on health matters. As such, it is a vital tool in the compilation of suicide statistics, analyses of suicide trends, and the development of suicide programs. WHO is one of the sponsors of World Suicide Prevention Day. The WHO website offers statistics on suicide and publishes research papers, studies, and a resource series called Preventing Suicide.

Bibliography of Books

Christian Baudelot and Roger Establet — *Suicide: The Hidden Side of Modernity*. Malden, MA: Polity Press, 2008.

Anat Berko — *The Path to Paradise: The Inner World of Suicide Bombers and Their Dispatchers*. Washington, DC: Potomac Books, 2009.

Kristine Bertini — *Understanding and Preventing Suicide: The Development of Self-Destructive Patterns and Ways to Alter Them*. Westport, CT: Praeger, 2009.

Jill Bialosky — *History of a Suicide: My Sister's Unfinished Life*. New York: Atria Books, 2011.

Dieter Birnbacher and Edgar Dahl, eds. — *Giving Death a Helping Hand: Physician-Assisted Suicide and Public Policy. An International Perspective*. Dordrecht, The Netherlands: Springer, 2008.

Ophir Falk and Henry Morgenstern, eds. — *Suicide Terror: Understanding and Confronting the Threat*. Hoboken, NJ: Wiley, 2009.

John E. Ferguson Jr. — *The Right to Die*. New York: Chelsea House Publishers, 2007.

Riaz Hassan — *Life as a Weapon: The Global Rise of Suicide Bombings*. New York: Routledge, 2010.

David Jeffrey — *Against Physician Assisted Suicide: A Palliative Care Perspective.* New York: Radcliffe, 2009.

Thomas Joiner — *Myths About Suicide.* Cambridge, MA: Harvard University Press, 2010.

Nancy Hartevelt Kobrin — *The Banality of Suicide Terrorism: The Naked Truth About the Psychology of Islamic Suicide Bombing.* Washington, DC: Potomac Books, 2010.

David Lester — *Preventing Suicide: Closing the Exits Revisited.* New York: Nova Science, 2009.

Jamshid A. Marvasti, ed. — *Psycho-Political Aspects of Suicide Warriors, Terrorism, and Martyrdom: A Critical View from "Both Sides" in Regard to Cause and Cure.* Springfield, IL: Charles C. Thomas, 2008.

Ariel Merari — *Driven to Death: Psychological and Social Aspects of Suicide Terrorism.* New York: Oxford University Press, 2010.

John B. Mitchell — *Understanding Assisted Suicide: Nine Issues to Consider.* Ann Arbor: University of Michigan Press, 2007.

Russell Razzaque — *Human Being to Human Bomb: Inside the Mind of a Terrorist.* Thriplow, England: Icon, 2008.

Leo Sher and Alexander Vilens, eds. — *Terror and Suicide.* New York: Nova Science, 2009.

Mary Warnock and Elisabeth MacDonald	*Easeful Death: Is There a Case for Assisted Dying?* New York: Oxford University Press, 2008.
John Weaver and David Wright, eds.	*Histories of Suicide: International Perspectives on Self-Destruction in the Modern World.* Toronto: University of Toronto Press, 2009.
John C. Weaver	*A Sadly Troubled History: The Meanings of Suicide in the Modern Age.* Montreal: McGill-Queen's University Press, 2009.

Index

Geographic headings and page numbers in **boldface** refer to viewpoints about that country or region.

CPSIA information can be obtained
at www.ICGtesting.com
Printed in the USA
FFOW040819151212
558FF